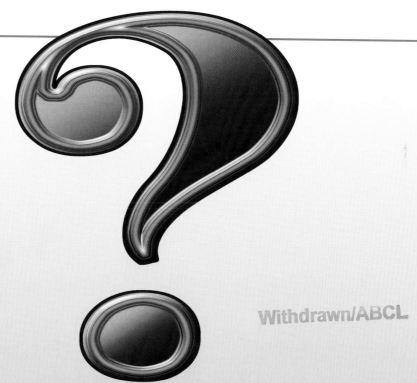

Always been a Babe and want to keep being one?

Never been a Babe and want to learn how?

Avoiding middle age?

Avoiding aging entirely?

Groping for your lost Babehood?

Below, specific, precise directions to become a fabulous Middle-Aged Babe.

HOW TO BE
A
MIDDLE-AGED
BABE

by

Marilyn Suzanne Miller

Illustrations by Karen Roston

Cover art by Karen Roston

Book design/graphics by Bob Pook

SCRIBNER

New York • London • Toronto • Sydney

DISCLAIMER

This publication is intended as a work of humor. It is sold with the understanding that the author and publisher are not engaged in rendering medical, health, or any other kind of personal professional services in the book. The reader should consult his or her medical, health, or other competent professional before adopting any of the suggestions in this book or drawing inferences from it.

The author and publisher specifically disclaim all responsibility for any liability, loss or risk, personal or otherwise, which is incurred as a consequence, directly or indirectly, of the use and application of any of the contents of this book.

SCRIBNER
A Division of Simon & Schuster, Inc.
1230 Avenue of the Americas
New York, NY 10020

SCRIBNER and design are trademarks of
Macmillan Library Reference USA, Inc., used under license
by Simon & Schuster, the publisher of this work.

First Scribner hardcover edition December 2007

For information about special discounts for bulk purchases,
please contact Simon & Schuster Special Sales at 1-800-456-6798
or business@simonandschuster.com

Illustrations by Karen Roston
Cover art by Karen Roston
Book design/graphics by Bob Pook
Text set in Times Roman

Manufactured in the United States of America

1   3   5   7   9   10   8   6   4   2

ISBN-13: 978-0-7432-9619-9
ISBN-10:   0-7432-9619-2

This book is dedicated to my phenomenal, gifted, loving mother,
Shirley M. Miller, writer/editor extraordinaire,
and to my much missed father, Dr. Norman R. Miller,
psychologist/jazz prodigy, who always started his best jokes
just as they put him under anesthesia.

MARILYN SUZANNE MILLER

CONTENTS

1. Introduction 1

2. What Is a "Middle-Aged Babe"? 11

GETTING THE LOOK

3. Middle-Aged Babe Essentials 19

4. Fitness (or "Thinness"): The Middle-Aged Babe's Guide to Exercise 33

5. Finances: Finances and the Middle-Aged Babe .41

6. Beauty 49

7. Plastic Surgery 61

8. Sex: You've Got Male: The Middle-Aged Babe's
   Complete Guide to Men 69

GETTING THE LIFE

9. Travel, Entertainment, and New Forms of Fun 93

10. Middle-Aged Babe Relationships: Old and New Friends,
    Boyfriends, Family, Extended Family, Overextended Family 111

11. Fat: A Global View 117

12. Health and the Middle-Aged Babe 135

13. The Middle-Aged Babe's Guide to Conception,
    Fertility, Menopause, and Contraception 139

14. From the Neck Up: The New Career Babe 159

15. Conclusions 165

    Acknowledgments 166

Photograph Credits

1. Introduction

What Is a Babe?

A Babe is the highest form of woman. With ample breasts (or the attitude of one who has ample breasts), a firm, assertive bottom (or a firm-bottom attitude), and long slinky hair, a babe is the state-of-the-art Hot Chick in America. Whether voluptuous or thin, svelte or buxom, she exudes man magnetism at age twenty or eighty.

And the Babe is complex. The highest form of Babe is both insightful *and* toned, firm *and* well-read, sultry *and* a giver to UNICEF.

Also, Babes are happier than other people, they can eat more, think harder, dance better, and they have big, great Babe attitudes. Indeed, Babehood has all to do with such attitude, what the French call "chien," a roguish, female charm.

Thus, while the true External Babe may be taut and curvy, the true Internal Babe can delight in a pair of farmer overalls while eating a huge, gooey s'more loudly in public.

Why? Because via language, demeanor, verve, and other intangibles, the true Babe gives off powerful Babe secretions that can rile a room of non-Babe women and under-Babed men, whether the practitioner is fifteen or sixty.

A Babe is taut, cool, cute, voluptuous or thin, friendly, hip, nice, and a good eater.

In short, a Babe is everything. She is happier, prettier, nicer, smarter, and better than all other people.

I Thought "Babes" Were Just "Hot." How Can I Be Both "Hot" and "Old"?

What do you mean by "old"? We didn't say anything about "old." You are "Middle" (or "Normal") Aged. We didn't say anything about old.

I Also Thought Babes Were Just Well-Endowed, Ego-Flaunting Sex Machines Who for Years Have Stared Out at Me from the Frames of Movies, from Across Living Rooms at Parties, and, Most Annoyingly, from Other Dressing Rooms in Stores, Shouting for Help in Their Ridiculously Tiny Thong Underwear, Smaller Than My Own by a Factor of Two or Four or a Million. I Hate Them! And Why Didn't You Mention I Could Be One of Them Before?

Because you couldn't. Middle Age, a restful, welcome break from real life, brings some unique opportunities.

Really?

Yes. It's a chance to grow spiritually, broaden mentally, and, most important, to reconfigure your concept of "Babehood." Many people like you mistakenly think Babes are just those thin, chic, sexy, abhorrently young women your husband eyes on the beach, your son ogles on MTV, and you see in magazine ads.*

Actually, such people are merely "Faux Babes," "Babe Poseurs," hollow Babe figurines who look like Babes but don't have the true Babe's passion or verve. In fact, the matter of "Who is a Babe?" (like "Who is a Jew?") can be very elusive. To examine this subject, let's have a brief quiz: Which of the following are Babes?

---

*And, sadly, it would follow that such anonymous, inconsequential, empty people—generally paid models—should set the standard for the way you are supposed to look and act in your real life. But, after all, this is America.

☐ Babe   ☐ Not a Babe

☐ Babe   ☐ Not a Babe

☐ Babe ☐ Not a Babe

Chaloner Woods/Hulton Archive/Getty Images

☐ Babe ☐ Not a Babe

☐ Babe ☐ Not a Babe

Diana Walker/Time & Life Pictures/Getty Images

☐ Babe ☐ Not a Babe

☐ Babe　　☐ Not a Babe

☐ Babe　　☐ Not a Babe

Keystone Features/Hulton Archive/Getty Images

OK, whatever your answers are, they were wrong. *Who knows what these people are like? These are just pictures.*

The fabulous-looking model with the bare midriff, for example, could be a GUY. Maybe she (he?) has good makeup, or surgery. Marilyn Monroe could even be a guy (especially here, this is just a photo). The staid, Victorian types could be Major Babes with Major Hair (once they untie it and lose the period costumes). And the one who's wearing the corset—she's probably a mannequin. The woman who looks so sad and the one on ice in the very brief dress? Both look a little nuts. And the Clintons—look at the eyes—you tell me: *Which is the Babe?* See how confused you are? Now let's consider your confusion about middle age.

What Is Middle Age?

The term *middle-aged,* invented by Descartes, comes from the Latin, *medeus,* meaning "not really old" and *ageis,* meaning "if you look at it in a certain way."

For decades, middle-aged was what your parents were, or what some other older, unpleasant people were. Now, is that what you are? Debate rages, for despite research, no outsider knows when a particular Babe's Middle Age starts or ends. And NO ONE uses the words "middle-aged" except to make a tragic point about themselves (for example: "I use a jeweler's loupe to read the classified ads, I guess that means I'm etc.," or "I used to be really thin, but now I'm etc.," or "I can't believe I'm pregnant because I'm etc.," or "I have zits and wrinkles, I guess I'm etc.").

Middle Age, then, has become the age which "dare not speak its name." It is (or was) the opposite of "cool" or "gorgeous" or "someone anyone wants to sleep with." Middle Age connotes fat, cancer, bad musical taste, and death. It conjures up a commuter in the sixties going to a Neil Simon play in Sans-abelt pants, a knit vest, balding, belly sagging—and then there's the men.

Widening waists, patio furniture, "making time in traffic"—this bespeaks the very special late-onset geekiness that beset our parents in postwar "middle age." Also, the very real possibility for you of growing fat as you near death and thus being seen by everyone while you are both DEAD AND FAT—don't tell me that's not the name of the tune on that little cassette, "The Middle-Aged Show!" you have stuck on "repeat" in your memory bank, blaring into your brain.

What Normally, in the Past, Has Happened to Babes in Middle Age?

Typically, in Middle Age, God has a little "makeover," like in fashion magazines, for women who allow things to just "go along" and make no effort to become "Middle-Aged Babes."

"God's Little Makeover" begins with little girls ("Before"), turns them into hot chicks ("After"), then, in middle age, plunges them into an "aging abyss" ("After That"). The "After That" state will happen to all women, whatever their race, religion, or national origin,* and is not yet enjoined against by the United Nations.

The prudent reader/Babe is advised: Take heed here of what happens, through the acute rudeness of aging, to all one-time Babes who don't use this book:

God's Little Makeover

Before

After

After That

---

*That is why there are so many people who look like the "After That" woman in our world and far fewer who look like the lovely creatures who precede them.

Before

After

After That

Before

After

After That

Before

After

After That

Before

After

After That

Before

After

After That

Before

After

After That

Now that wasn't pretty, was it?

Hey, Excuse Me, but the "Babes" Here All Look Incredibly Young. How Can a Babe Be Middle-Aged?

Let's first look at what you call "young," or "The New Youth."

What is Youth Now?

Youth is now a teeny, tiny, hard-to-locate segment of time between "Baby" and "Other" (see figure (a)). Two influences have caused this reconfiguring of Youth. One, the earlier onset of puberty in girls (due to obvious influences: the environment, TV, music, the gravity of world circumstance, the pre-eminence of the stiletto heel and halter top, and the effect of other biological swift-aging or "olding" factors on the young). The other is the extended life span of the relentlessly, ruthlessly young Baby Boom, eighty million people aging fast as comets, but showing it less, indeed refusing to age, unless they get a disease and die, and sometimes not even then.

These two influences—the eminent stiletto, and the almost-dead-but-young Baby Boomers—have had an "olding" effect on the young, and a "younging" effect on the whole population. Few people are still classically "young"; indeed, the new "Late Youth" and "Old Youngness" have ballooned our once flat, smooth, yes, teenlike demographic midriff, to include almost everyone cool (see figure (a) below).

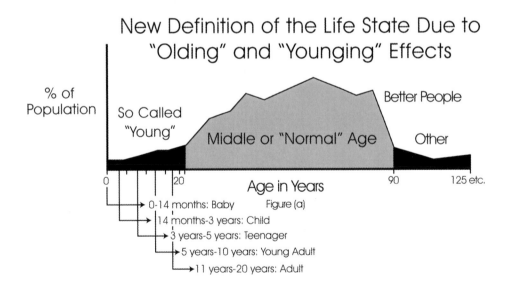

New Definition of the Life State Due to "Olding" and "Younging" Effects

Figure (a)

Youth, then, once ballyhooed as the epicenter of fun, hot dogs, hot sex, and marvelous dope-smoking good times, is now defined as follows: that period before death, characterized by smooth skin and ill-formed ideas. And indeed, as anyone can see by talking to a typical, deeply annoyed thirteen-year-old: from twenty-one on, we are all middle-aged.

(*Note:* The new "Late Youth" or "Old Youngness" can also be seen in two critical areas sociologists have noted: "current birth patterns" and "patterns of wearing cropped tops." Women are having children later and later in life *and* wearing cropped tops earlier and earlier, in a large, frightening demographic which, if unchecked, could result in cropped tops that are more and more cropped, being worn at ages that are less and less cropped, by frankly, very old, pregnant women, an unhappy sight in anyone's book (see figure (b) below).

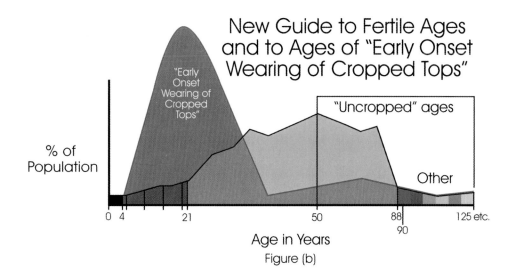

Figure (b)

But What About Those Expressions We Still Hear So Often, "Young Babe" or "Hot Young Babe" or "Hey, Look at That Hot Young Babe!"? Never, "Oh, Look At That Middle-Aged Babe!"

Oh, please! No one will say that "Hot Young Babe" thing any more, as there is clearly now no such thing as being hot while young (see parameters of "Young People," figure (a)). Middle-Aged Babes will naturally be called in to take up the "Hot" slack.

Common Pitfalls of the "Hot Young Babe"

"Younger Middle-Aged Babes," as they will now be known, are often late (with their periods and otherwise). They can be confused by the difference between love and lust (a particular horror to men). They are also confused about events of the day, events of the sixties, and the difference between the fifties and sixties, and are also too fast bike riders. Most critically, some have "radiant PMS," PMS of such profound dimension that it radiates, causing fullness, bloating, and irritability in innocent passersby! Middle-Aged Babes, however, often are lucky enough* to have no period at all. They are smart, nice, beautiful, and some can park really close to anywhere, as they have the sexiest asset a Middle-Aged Man can imagine: a Handicapped parking sticker.

---

* Because they are so cute.

Why Was There No Such Thing as "The Middle-Aged Babe" Previously?

Past generations felt women should just "grow old gracefully." Given the medical climate then, of course, all one could do as one got old was just "grow" that way: one simply "ran out" of youth. Life, then, had an "old" and a "young," but virtually no "middle." "Middle Age" was just the sad, short portal a woman whizzed through on her way to Old Age. "Gracefully" was the one ladylike route to a final decline, the most dignified way to drag oneself off the planet.

Today, lifespans have grown such that "Middle Age" is a significant new period, so long it is comparable to *Remembrance of Things Past* or a Hip-Hop star's limo. With medical research, Middle Age has become a kinetic, fruitful time filled with greater energy, enhanced good looks, mental acuity, emotional *and* physical well-being. Middle Age, a new chunk of "Earth Time," a gift of new "life real estate," affords chances to change, pursue the new, and become way, totally happening.

You may be in denial about Middle Age as a category you are in, saying things like, "Fifty is the new Thirty," never going to the eye doctor, preferring to have all your ophthalmic needs met by the Wal-Mart reading glasses displays. Your birthday parties may be characterized by an odd, *total* omission of candles from the cake! Moreover, you may also *still insist on having babies, even as your eggs come down your Fallopian tubes on crutches every month (if they show up at all)!* True, you may force conception (via in vitro, etc.) *while* secretly reading pamphlets on menopause in the gynecologist's waiting room. Sound familiar? The New Middle Age is a chance to grow spiritually, broaden mentally, get some plastic surgery or unpleasant, painful "beauty injections" (optional), and, in all ways, to revivify your sagging self and life.

"Oh, sure," you say. But perhaps *first* ask, "How good could a *Middle-Aged* Babe possibly be?"

2. What Is a "Middle-Aged Babe"?

The Middle-Aged Babe is a new, deep, rich form of Babe. She combines the stylish wearability of a regular Babe with the durability of a good used car. She is a rich, full-bodied Babe, incredibly sexy, having come through these days of new bacteria and terrorist attacks with one of the sexiest things one can have: a long life span (this the Middle-Aged Babe *demonstrably* has, having *actually reached* Middle Age).

She knows Middle Age not as the Kiss-Off Age it once was, a lifestyle cul-de-sac, but rather a "lifestyle major intersection" filled with delightful "happiness off ramps" and "enrichment on ramps."

Middle Age, once a despised spot to be avoided, is the new "Destination Age."

Clever catch phrases like "donor eggs," "mini–face lift," and "chemo and radiation" expand the fun-having envelope of the Middle-Aged Babe with an increased reach of motherhood, anticancer treatment, and beauty—often occurring all at once!

Never before have Babes lived so long, had such cool jobs, or shots at "cool second jobs." And second lives.

Faux Woes Over

With the faux woes of youth behind her, the Middle-Aged Babe can have the shiny exterior of a "Hot Young Babe" without its unshiny interior, for the Middle-Aged Babe sees her physical person not as some Temple to Aging (although she is free to do so), but as a fab value on the body real estate market, a possible teardown she is willing to entirely renovate, via a doctor—or herself! (See "Plastic Surgery You Can Do at Home," page 63.)

Unlike the outré "Hot Young Babe," the Middle-Aged Babe is not sulking—not morose over her eye shadow color, nor asking if you think she's fat, if you think *other* people do, or asking how fat she is compared to passing strangers. Why? *Because she knows she is fat, is on a diet, or couldn't care less!*

Highest Form of Babe

As the Babe is the highest form of woman, so the Middle-Aged Babe is the highest form of Babe, its best model, the "Hummer 2 Babe," with great new features. She knows doctors, knows doctors' specialties, knows what "doctors' specialties" means, *knows doctors' home phone numbers*, looks great in a slit skirt and mules, and *doesn't waste time having an eventful inner life* (see "Hot Young Babe," above).

And the Middle-Aged Babe is prettier, wittier, more accomplished, and better than all preceding categories of Babe. Not sadder but wiser—she is Sadder but Happier! Why? Because *the Middle-Aged Babe has been through shit and knows what to do with it: Get over it! Now!*

Previous versions of Babes evolved into the current model, "The Middle-Aged Babe." And all men converge on her—true, she may be short a few body parts (the Mastectobabe), but, again—think of all the doctors she knows!

The Middle-Aged Babe has attitude, joy, courage, a great butt, and, if you are the man of her dreams or of the hour, is delighted to go to nonchick flicks with you, and to widen your and her sexual parameters, with proper negotiations.*

So How Does One Get to Be a Middle-Aged Babe? I Can Do the Middle-Aged Part Myself. How About the "Babe"?

Babehood occurs on a cellular level. It is now known these cells can be altered through an exciting new method: TRYING! "Babehood" develops from a naturally occurring inner-body "girly clay" (amino acid) in the cell nuclei, which must be coaxed, cajoled, pressed, yelled at, and kicked into Babehood.

Maladaptive Mistake

Not becoming a Middle-Aged Babe would be THE inconceivable maladaptive mistake of midlife, like refusing to become a butterfly when you've been a caterpillar, or not evolving into Man when you've finished being a dreadful pile of slowly evolving sludge for a zillion years. Oh, sure, you can mire in the do-nothingness that is the "Old Middle Age," signing for deliveries, listening to *Car Talk* on NPR—*those* can be your highs. Or you can become a Middle-Aged Babe, the sane Early/Late Female Life State of Choice.

Discipline Required

Still, Babehood is a discipline requiring lifestyle adjustment. Fashion magazines and self-help books have a smug, doctrinaire, clothes-pushing, know-it-all, heavy-handed attitude toward personal improvement. Well, *How to Be a Middle-Aged Babe* has a worse attitude, *more* smug and doctrinaire. *Our* "tips" are to be followed slavishly with no thought to your needs and feelings or those of your family. We expect you to happily rework your old self to within an inch of its life, to rethink every piece of you, as if a thousand pieces have fallen on the floor from a huge canister of Legos, and you are the Legos.

---

* And will not ask what you think of her eye shadow color while doing it.

Deviate, and fall short of the glory inherent in being a Middle-Aged Babe: with a glow in midlife irreducible by ages ending in zero or five, by divorce, disease, or endless "global aggravation," via a sort of "Babes-only" ecstasy. This comes via little-known, new Middle-Aged Babe products *revealed here for the first time,* like:

- Raloxitox—Raloxifene mixed with Botox, to plump wrinkles. Together, they're injected into the face as a hot flash-coolant–wrinkle-buster, all in one!
- The new Middle-Aged Babe Compensatory Underwear, designed to lift, separate, compress, and totally redirect the traffic of every part of your body.
- Learn pointers on all-new Middle-Aged Babe Fun: binge living, staying awake, swinging hard before 9 p.m., etc.
- Enjoy the Middle-Aged Babe's Metabolic Enhancer CD—lie down and listen to stressful stories about terrifying things (your name inserted in each!) to raise your heart rate and metabolic level *while you sleep.*
- The Middle-Aged Babe's Guide to Longer Legs.
- "Panic Investing—Why It Works: Our Model Midlife Portfolio."
- Also—"Sex: You've Got Male!: The Middle-Aged Babe's Complete Guide to Men" instructs: "How to Tell if You Are Married or Single," a complete guide to oral sex, and, for the forgetful Babe, a tear-out poster to hang in your closet for help in oral sex emergencies!
- Also for the (surprisingly still-able-to-get-pregnant Perimenopausal Babe): "All-New Instructions on How to Insert a Diaphragm" and (if you fail) "Breast Pumps in Restaurants: When Are They Right?"
- "From the Neck Up: The New Career Babe."
- On Travel: "Getting a Rush from Going Where State Department Travel Advisories Urge You to Avoid"!
- Plus: "The Middle-Aged Babe's Guide to Terrifying New Medical Tests."

What could be hotter?

A Final Note

Ancient mapmakers, drawing oceans and seas, wrote, where the world flattened to its "edge," "Yonder There Be Dragons." This is how many of us have thought of middle age, the time we are no longer "Babes."

Crossing the Miss/Ma'am Transit

The Miss/Ma'am Transit begins at the point a sixteen-year-old bag boy at a grocery checkout suddenly, for the first time, calls you "ma'am" instead of "miss."

If this is followed by a *second* sixteen-year-old bag boy calling you "ma'am" within one (1) year, you have crossed the Miss/Ma'am Transit and entered into the period of Middle Age, in which, *devoid of any Middle-Aged Babe elements,* there will, in fact, be dragons.

This is the cause of understandable upset. Wildly fluctuating EEGs have been recorded at this moment, in readings done by research teams hunched behind grocery checkouts worldwide. As reconstructed by researchers, a general perception of this moment looks as follows:

Diagram of "Crossing the Miss/Ma'am Transit"

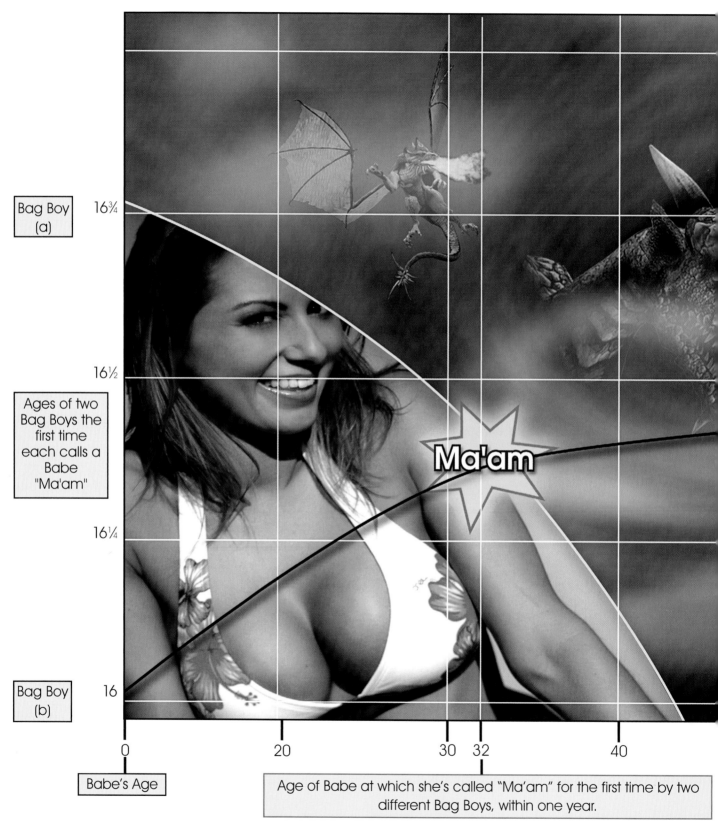

Bag Boy (a) 16¾

16½

Ages of two Bag Boys the first time each calls a Babe "Ma'am"

16¼

Ma'am

Bag Boy (b) 16

0   20   30 32   40

Babe's Age

Age of Babe at which she's called "Ma'am" for the first time by two different Bag Boys, within one year.

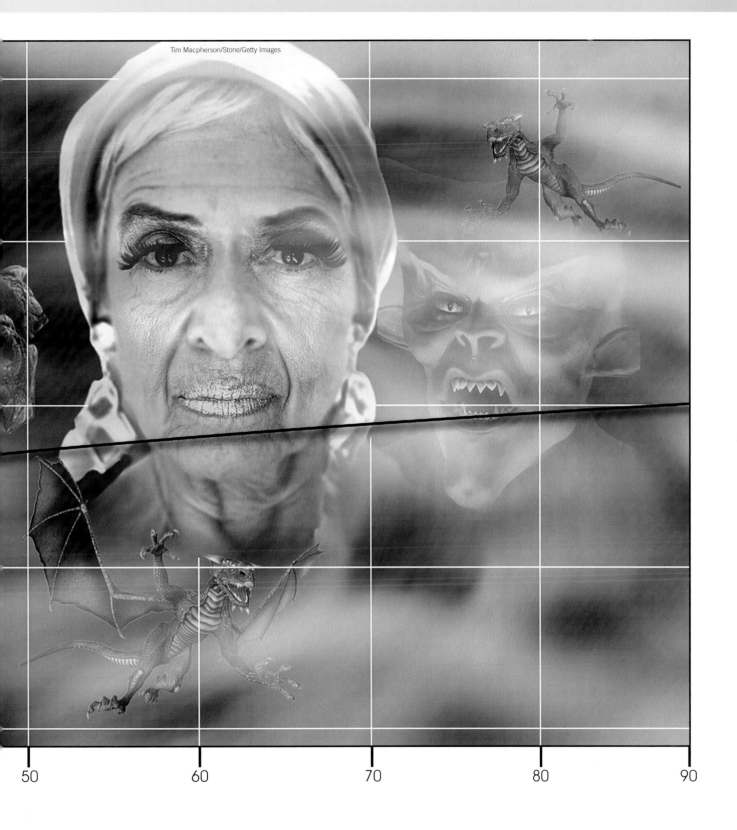

Tim Macpherson/Stone/Getty Images

50   60   70   80   90

Region in Conflict: Why You Must Be a Middle-Aged Babe

Middle Age is an opportunity age. Today, worthwhile shows on TV are named things like "Region in Conflict." Others are "Nation in Crisis," "Threat from Within," "Our Terrifying Lives," "Acres and Acres of Conflict," "CNN Is Frightened," "Crisis in Peril," and "Get Out of Your House Now!" You will watch these shows. *Do you want to watch them as a willfully, joyous Babe or as a person with nothing else going on?*

Studies show Middle-Aged Babes have appreciably lower blood pressure and potato chip intake during "World Fear Today" or "CNN Is Frantic" than any other group.

So, if you're going to watch "Region in Conflict"—and you are—watch it as a Middle-Aged Babe.

GETTING
THE
LOOK

3. Middle-Aged Babe Essentials

Babehood raises the languidly aging middle-aged female to a vigorous death-sluffing, gene-defying beauty, inside and out. However, Middle-Aged Babehood is both intrinsic and demonstrable, implied and stated: *all these traits, then, must be represented by the "Babe on View."*

Achieving the Optimum "Babe on View"

The Essentials are "requisite components of exterior Babehood," designed to begin construction of the exterior Middle-Aged Babe (e.g., "Babe on View").

Creating this Exterior Babe is crucial, because by decking the Outer Babe, the Inner Babe will surely follow. The Outer Babe, in fact, may sweep the reticent Inner Nonbabe off her feet into the arms of adventure, sexiness, beauty, nonfiction books, and hip, new invasive medical tests.

First Tier
Middle-Aged Babe Essentials

The first (and most essential) Middle-Aged Babe Essentials are: Easy Go Separates, sunglasses, a gynecological exam gown (with ties), a camisole, an X-ray gown, "happy shoes" (low-heeled mules), "nude under anything," a choir (or choir-type) robe (to slip on at times of sudden weight gain and announce, "I'm off to choir practice!"), cleavage (or cleavage equivalent; a cleavage-type product), the full lip (or full-lip attitude), a mammography gown (which may be set on fire right after the test), an easy, comfy sexual position, a birthing gown (for Younger Middle-Aged Babes and Middle-Aged Babes pushing the conception envelope), and anything from Harley (except, of course, a Harley).

Also: dressy underpants, comfy underpants, comfy At-Home Loungewear, comfy mules, Jimmy Choo–like Sling-Backs, a midriff-baring cropped top,* jeans in "How Fat Today?" categories, Day-into-Evening Purse, a soufflé-begetting eggbeater, a "Go Anywhere" tiara, and, last—"visible Babe attitude" (see chick photo shown—bravado, swagger, *joie, je ne sais quoi*—these English and French things can be faked at first, but will act on others till they act on you). Also, for Plastic Surgery You Can Do at Home: scissors, a hot glue gun, embroidery hoops, and three-way mirror.

Any three of these Essentials will shout "Hey, here's a Babe!" even at (particularly at) middle age.

Examples:

Full Lips + Choir Robe + Major Babe Attitude = Middle-Aged Babe

Hot Glue Gun + Anything Harley + Dressy Underpants = Middle-Aged Babe

Mammogram Gown + Comfy At-Home Loungewear + Go Anywhere Tiara = Middle-Aged Babe

Eggbeater + Scissors + Easy, Comfy Sexual Position = Middle-Aged Babe

Et cetera

---

* Where Babe midriff justifies use only.

Middle-Aged Babe Essentials

Easy Go Separates

Anything Harley

Camisole

Go Anywhere Cropped Top

Cleavage

Jimmy Choo–Like Sling-Backs

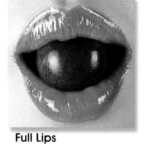

Full Lips

Major Babe Attitude

Happy Shoes

Sunglasses

a. Mammography Gown
b. X-ray Gown
c. Gynecological Gown
d. Choir-type Robe

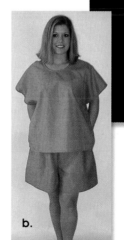

a.

b.

c.

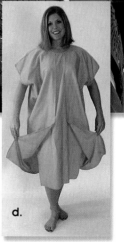

d.

Evan Agostini/Getty Images Entertainment

Middle-Aged Babe Essentials

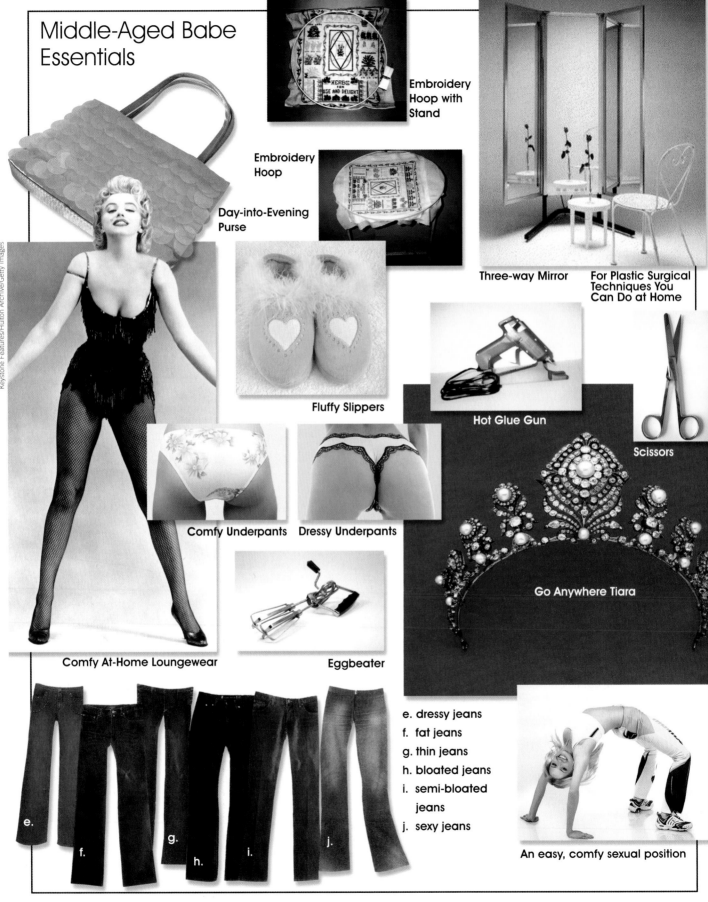

Embroidery Hoop with Stand

Embroidery Hoop

Day-into-Evening Purse

Three-way Mirror

For Plastic Surgical Techniques You Can Do at Home

Fluffy Slippers

Hot Glue Gun

Scissors

Comfy Underpants

Dressy Underpants

Go Anywhere Tiara

Comfy At-Home Loungewear

Eggbeater

e. dressy jeans
f. fat jeans
g. thin jeans
h. bloated jeans
i. semi-bloated jeans
j. sexy jeans

e.
f.
g.
h.
i.
j.

An easy, comfy sexual position

Keystone Features/Hulton Archive/Getty Images

22

Second Tier
Middle-Aged Babe Essentials:
Compensatory Underwear

Any "Wardrobe of Babe Affect" must, of course, enfold the Middle-Aged Babe body and contain compensations for the flesh. It must right the Middle-Aged Babe's figure and any drawbacks it may, surprisingly, have. This can be done with some goal-oriented, unique "developmental underwear." The Middle-Aged Babe is, of course, not just in some random body that she leaves to its own devices, sending it out for the evening, believing it's adequate. No, the Middle-Aged Babe Bod, fallen into disrepair, is often an "anatomical teardown" requiring constant gutting, reducing, adding of wings (and breasts), reduction of anterooms (and thighs). It takes time for Babe Total Body Reclamation. Also effort, exercise, diet. In fact, generally, it may never happen at all.

Thus, we present here The Middle-Aged Babe's Compensatory Underwear. Unlike regular underwear, which foolishly allows you to be yourself, the Middle-Aged Babe's Compensatory Underwear cleverly, through a series of pulleys, ramps, mice running in turnstiles, and hydroelectric cinches, fashions you into what we all know to be the optimum physical being: someone else. No one can know the joy of this better than the Middle-Aged Babe, especially when this marvelous "other person's body" is her own. Instantly available from a catalog, or online to be FedExed to you immediately, this "compensatory underwear" lifts spirits, encourages "inner-tissue effort," and cannot be done without. (See Appendix A for order forms.)

Extreme "Thinness": Apply Elsewhere!

We emphasize: The Middle-Aged Babe *need not* be the culturally acclaimed "thin." She may just require minor flesh tweaks here and there to better endow her " Babe Essentials" wardrobe. And while this may be more rambunctious underwear than you're used to, isn't that exactly the problem? Other, less caring underwear—the notably laid-back, frilly lingerie department underwear—simply allow Babe parts to slide into the grip of gravity without redress! Here, then, for the impending Babe who wants a quick Faux-Toned Start-Up Bod, we present "Middle-Aged Babe Compensatory Underwear," as lovely as it is transforming.

The Thigh Retainer

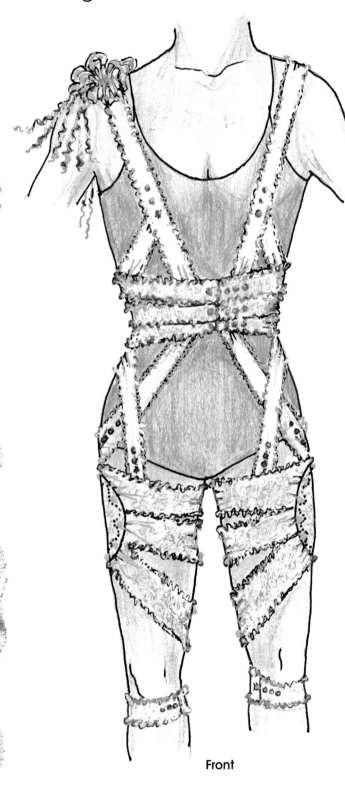

Front

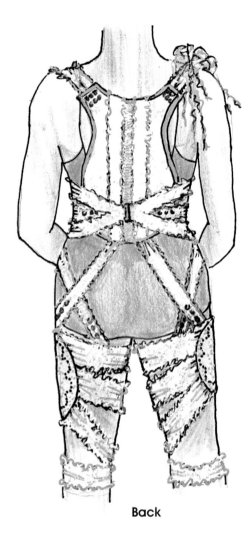

Back

Created with delightful silk plissé stretch lace Ace bandage–like panels, the "thigh retainer" lifts "outer-upper thigh" with reinforced, boned hernia-girdle latex support orbs. These industrial-grade spandex "plates" flatten and lift, with shoulder-to-knee supports held tight by a charming crepe de Chine silk georgette/asbestos pitcher's chest pad (worn backward), riveted with organdy airplane grommets at three different settings. One size fits all.

The Buttock Fluffer Upper

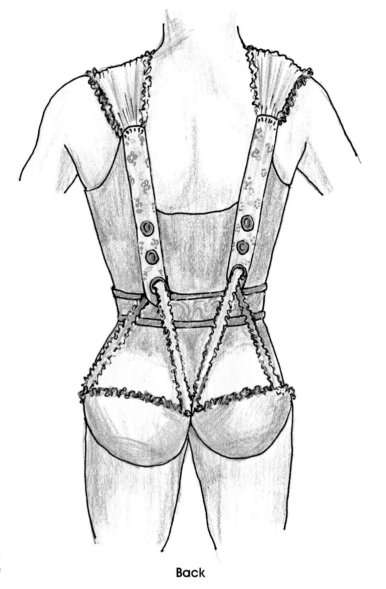

Back

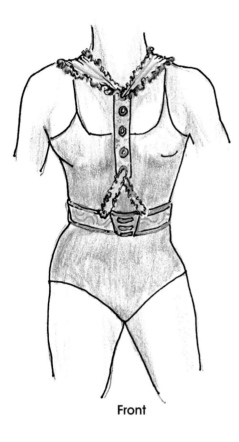

Front

Stretch lace and embroidered pastel damask-charmeuse straps support an "underwire panty," which may be raised or lowered through silk grommets, threading them higher or lower, front and back. Anchored by a Gold's Gym–inspired weight-lifting belt, done in lush patterned duchesse silk satin, trimmed in ruched silk satin bouclé, it slims waist and anchors rear weight (with ruffled eyelet crepe flounce). Buttocks may be ratcheted up or down.

The Mammary Sling

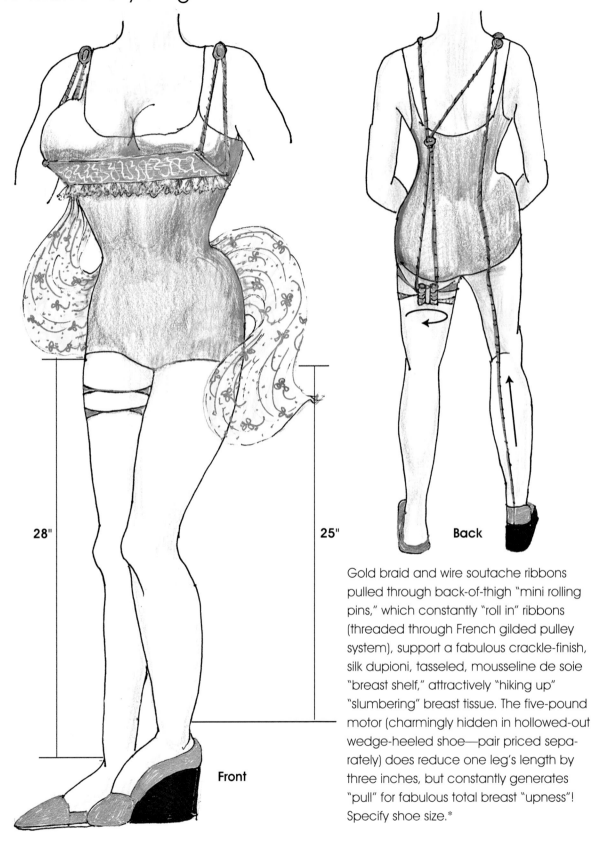

28"

25"

Back

Front

Gold braid and wire soutache ribbons pulled through back-of-thigh "mini rolling pins," which constantly "roll in" ribbons (threaded through French gilded pulley system), support a fabulous crackle-finish, silk dupioni, tasseled, mousseline de soie "breast shelf," attractively "hiking up" "slumbering" breast tissue. The five-pound motor (charmingly hidden in hollowed-out wedge-heeled shoe—pair priced separately) does reduce one leg's length by three inches, but constantly generates "pull" for fabulous total breast "upness"! Specify shoe size.*

* Lacy hydroelectric purse motor also available. Price by request.

The Abs Inducer

Detail of Power Drive

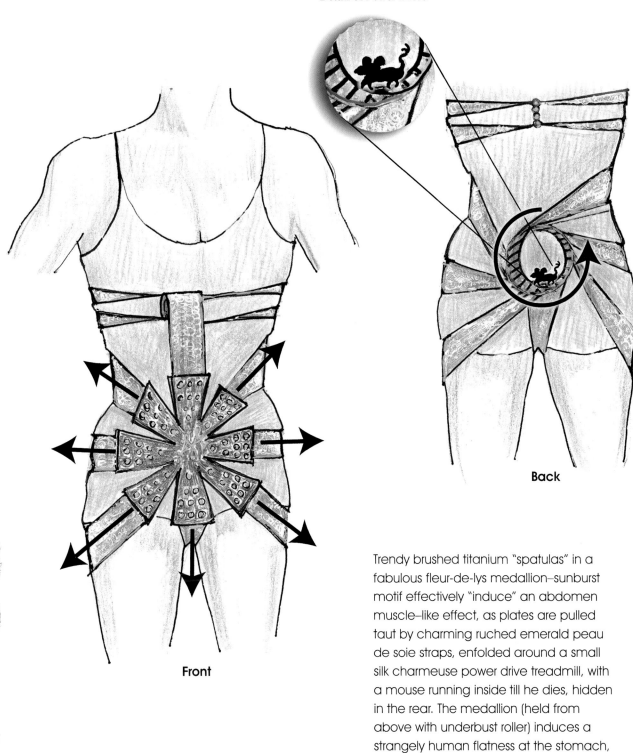

Back

Front

Trendy brushed titanium "spatulas" in a fabulous fleur-de-lys medallion–sunburst motif effectively "induce" an abdomen muscle–like effect, as plates are pulled taut by charming ruched emerald peau de soie straps, enfolded around a small silk charmeuse power drive treadmill, with a mouse running inside till he dies, hidden in the rear. The medallion (held from above with underbust roller) induces a strangely human flatness at the stomach, as if the abdominal muscles were actually still there.

The Chin Corrector Blouse

Crisp white oxford cloth collar "completely hides" "totally invisible," semi–flesh-colored molded plastic neck restraint bars, "invisibly" lifts chin and neck, fits discreetly over ears with "invisible" over-ear harnesses; keeps neck and chin flesh taut by pressing the full weight of the head directly into the sternum. (Pressure on sternum may be relieved by removing plastic pins, which *may* puncture skin. Undetectable!) Adjusts with rear ear snaps.

Third Tier
Middle-Aged Babe Essentials:
All Black Clothes

For decades, all black clothes have been de rigueur for offhand chic. (In New York, All Black's Low-Maintenance *soignée* made it the city's Babe Signature Look.) Recently, profit-distracted designers generated a surge of embellished color, thinking it would be "bought" and create a "profit" in a "store." But for Middle-Aged Babes, black rules: it's understated, it's day, it's evening, it's not at all like a nun's habit, and it travels from poolside to mammography with panache. Black and black is the emblem of Metropolitan Hip.

But Blacks vary. Like any other two colors, black and black must be put together carefully—a midnight black blazer won't work worn over a "film noir" black poncho. Nor should Babes throw a black "deep anthracite" cashmere shawl over a "midnight charcoal" wetsuit. The Middle-Aged Babe populace, heavily invested in black, will wear it. (Add color via "Hi! I'm ———" stickers or (high-end) colored diamonds from Bergdorf's. Hermès anything, *especially the shopping bag,* that delightful, crisp orange paper tote, carried daily for the rest of your life, lends tony flash to any look.) But exactly how to coordinate a look that works?

Here, the Middle-Aged Babe's "Mix 'n' Match All Black Wardrobe Guide," our tone-on-tone bible.

The Middle-Aged Babe's Mix 'n' Match
All Black Wardrobe Guide

1+5

6+8+1

4+7+8

1+6+9

1+5

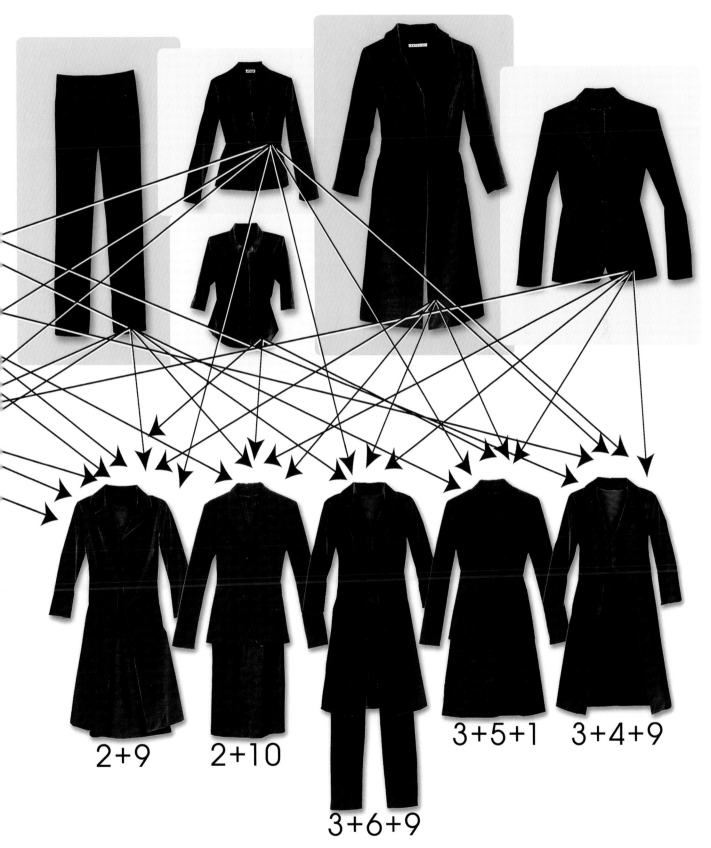

2+9

2+10

3+6+9

3+5+1

3+4+9

4. Fitness (or "Thinness")
The Middle-Aged Babe's Guide to Exercise

The Middle-Aged Babe craves Fitness (or "Thinness"). "Fitness" is, of course, equivalent to "Thinness" (indeed, it is alternately recognized as such, a synonym). And why not? America, an advanced, modern society which proudly invented bulimia, clearly looks upon them as the same thing. Fitness ("Thinness") lowers blood pressure, reduces bad cholesterol, and helps vital organs, like the heart, lungs, thighs, and behind.

Assuring her "Fitness" ("Thinness") is crucial to the Middle-Aged Babe, who takes care of her body: exercises, smokes when the body demands it, and practices rigorous "inner tissue surveillance" (via doctor visits, or tiny inner-tissue security guards with teensy-weensy security cameras she has installed in her capillaries by Brinks/Mt. Sinai Hospital). Thus, the "Fitness/Thinness" duality is not a problem for the tissue-savvy Babe who knows that to be attractive, she must look good everywhere, in a swimsuit, evening gown, tennis match, *and* on the operating table.

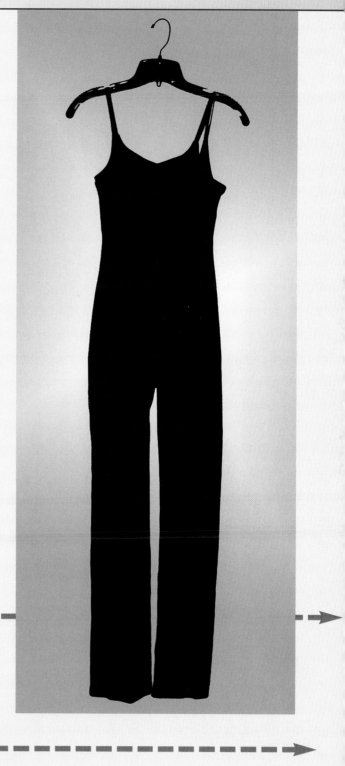

Exercise

No Babe cares for exercise, though she may do it fanatically. The wise Babe knows exercise for what it is, simply a "danced diet," causing "Fitness" ("Thinness") as a charming by-product, like a trip to France may produce a Hermès bag.

New Alternatives

There are new exercise options for the Middle-Aged Babe discussed here. There's one surprisingly effective form of extremely low-low-impact exercise known as the Middle-Aged Babe's Aerobic Tableau. Other great new exercise-surrogates: the Portable Strap-on Midriff (see "Essentials: Tier One," Appendix A) and the Middle-Aged Babe's Guide to Crunch-Free Abs (from AAA, to be done while driving, coming soon!).

Cardiovascular Noblesse Oblige

The Middle-Aged Babe strives, of course, not simply to be "Fit" but admired for her Fitness ("Thinness") by others. She wants not just Cardiovascular Wellness, or Cardiovascular Greatness but Cardiovascular Noblesse Oblige, telling less Fit friends not only how few days she works out lately but what short, negligent distances she runs once in a blue moon. (For true Cardiovascular Noblesse Oblige, a Babe must have run like a banshee for years and exercised in constant 24-hour cycles.)

Note: Slovenly Babes *benefit* when all riled up envying other people's Fitness, *as envy is aerobic.* It gets Babe pulses pumping with heart-pounding envy, and soon they're shedding pounds like the svelte people's persons they covet (as we'll see later in "The Middle-Aged Babe's Guide to the Cardiovascular Benefits of Envy," Appendix B).

The Wish to Keep One's Original Body

Many Middle-Aged Babes wistfully recall the forties or fifties, when your body was just some *body* you got, not today's flesh edifice, an "anatomical teardown" to which you must ever add amenities like muscle tone, stamina, and maybe, one fine day, central vacuum and his and her bidets (rumored even now to be housed in the body cavities of Goldie Hawn and Barbra Streisand). For most Babes, the "inner-body rosewood sauna" is still only a dream.

Two Types of Middle-Aged Babes: The "Never Exercised" and "Ever Exercised"

The Never Exercised or "Lummox-Style" Babe needs motivation, never having had endorphins pleasurably marinate her brain.

Endorphins are mostly gay hormones, which, released via exercise, run through the corridors of the Babe's mind in drag, sliding on the mind's highly polished floors in their socks, drinking blue margaritas, making phony phone calls, fixing each other's hair, and doing the hoochie-coochie dance in their underpants, throughout her psychological underpinnings. This rare natural high is acceded to ordinarily only on one's wedding night or at the Saks Designer Consolidation Sale.

The "Ever Exercised" Babe, always at the high school track, Jazzercise, Lotte Berk, and Pilates for decades, is sick of inner tissue servicing. Thus, the Exercised Babe's weary of exercise, and the Logy Babe, dulled by inactivity, is weary of weariness. Both sloth and jock share a zero tolerance policy toward fat *and* death, calling for some efficient new "fast but slow," "easy but hard," "painful but pleasant," midlife exercise routine.

New Requirements

The Middle-Aged Babe requires a sort of Post-Ted-Turner-Jane-Fonda Workout, something brief yet triumphant, resulting in firm thighs and an incredible financial settlement, done in a couple of hours or less in a courthouse in Atlanta (or its equivalent). No leg lifts, as the Babe now sees leg lifts for what they are—the indefensible Electoral College of exercise where a hundred million leg lifts represent one-eighteenth of an inch of fat gone.

What Is "Aerobics" or "Aerobic Exercise"?

Aerobics compress, then stretch the muscles rapidly, so the heart pumps harder, recirculating blood into the muscles; muscles compress, stretch faster (raise metabolism even *after* exercise). Now, *what if this same thing were done, but with your bones?* Impossible? Exactly. Perfect for the Babe's "major over-achiever" heart.

The Middle-Aged Babe's Stationary Whiplash: All New!

For the Babe's conceited heart, we introduce an aerobic first: "The Middle-Aged Babe's Full Bone Workout."

This new "bone stretch" is so effective Babes feel it in their back, legs, and hair. The main "bone flex" (or "Middle-Aged Babe's Aerobic Spinal Crunch," "Stationary Back Flip," or "Vertebral Yank") pulls the spine into a wonderful "Stationary Whiplash," creating opposing pressures and stretches within *and between* the spinal column *and* lower back muscles (like in a war), achieving a wonderful multi-muscle "spinal attack" where the spine is clenched, vertebrae crushed, then relaxed (if they are not smooshed or completely dislocated).

How It Works!

Spinal bones (especially after this exercise) often don't have blood-supplying capillaries. Thus, the big ego heart will just work harder, impossibly, crazily hard, to induce the response it gets with muscles, raising metabolism gloriously. With no response, the confused, depressed heart *may* just give up, sulk, and stop entirely (a small risk). We believe Babe Hearts are far too conceited to quit. Thus, the "full bone workout," way harder and more fabulously inhumane than anything, will burn fat unprecedentedly, on the Babe herself and those standing near her!

"Tibia contractions," "rib clenches," and "funny bone pulses" follow for the Babe as she advances. (Suggestion: While squeezing the sacral muscles against the vertebrae, and smashing the vertebrae into each other, cheer for one side or the other, whichever is winning!! Such "team tension" works well in competitive sports, why not *within your own* body?)

Learning By Doing!

Let's see how the "Vertebral Smoosh" or humorously nicknamed "Herniated Disc Widowmaker" lets the Middle-Aged Babe do in ten minutes what would otherwise take years with a whining, annoyingly thin trainer.

We're proud that the Middle-Aged Babe Aerobic Spinal Crunch is the first advance in the aerobic life of the spinal cord, and the first-ever exercise use of the herniated (or soon to be herniated) disc.

We start with a Beginner's version, appropriate for any Babe who owns some spandex; as shown, it uses only the most elementary "spinal crunches" and "spinal lunges." We strongly assert: Babes mustn't try this program without exercise background, medical approval, and showing the routine to your doctor! Do "reps" *only where indicated,* repeat sequence twenty minutes a day, checking pulse after the first five.* A good Beginner's "first small step."

Beginners

"The Middle-Aged Babe's Beginner's Aerobic/Spinal Workout" is for the Babe with substantial training. It should not be done more than twenty minutes a day, requires "pulse checks," and should be copied in strict sequence. Precede with "pre-spinal-clench warm-ups," "pre-spinal-warm-up clench clenches," and "cranial lunges" (to reduce hard-to-reach head fat). The Middle-Aged Babe must "warm up" as if her life ("physical beauty") depended on it. (It does!) The "warm-up," with "vertebral clenches," "disc head-locks," and "cervical spasms," is followed by the workout. A Fitness ("Thinness") first for the Babe to spring to good health ("good looks").

A great "First Step" for the newly "re-exercising" Babe.

---

* Count heartbeats for fifteen seconds, multiply by four, see chart, "Appropriate height/weight/age/pulse rates for Middle-Aged Babes," Appendix C, and (compulsory): *first check with your medical doctor for your max spinal/CPR rates!*

The Middle-Aged Babe's
Beginner's Aerobic/Spinal Workout

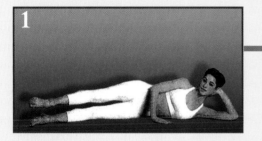

1. Lying on side, tuck coccyx (base of spine) firmly between buttocks. Press upper leg up ten times, till you feel a stretch in the hip; keep spinal cord relaxed.
2. Suddenly, clench your vertebral discs together, pressing the spine hard against itself, so hard it draws the body up into a backwards curl. Hold, clench discs tighter and tighter. Relax. Clench discs. Relax. Clench.
3. Force vertebrae together so hard it squirts you up onto your feet. Kick right leg up, keeping spine loose.

4. Clench spine; then, using the force of the base of the spine, pull the back to floor, lie with legs in V.
5. Use spine to push off floor, catapult to a flying gazelle position. Hold.
6. Slam to floor knee first, merging your discs in a full spinal arch, pushing discs harder and harder against one another, listening for a "fender bender" or cracked knuckles sound. Allow cracked knuckles sound to become louder, like the sound of someone playing castanets, or smashing acorns under their foot. Hold.

7. Spring to a demi-plié position. Bounce.
8. Snap spine back suddenly with a force that smashes you to the floor knee first, discs in a full Stationary Backflip. Listen for cracked knuckles or fender bender sound. "Power back-bend," spine together so hard, it pushes head to the floor.
9. Stand lightly on your head. Relax.

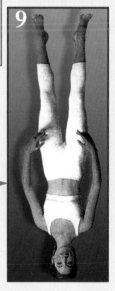

The Middle-Aged Babe's
Advanced Beginner's Aerobic/Spinal Workout*

* Consult your physician before beginning any exercise program.

Wow!

What effortless, novel, fun physical tyranny! Can Fitness ("Thinness") be far behind?

In upcoming editions we hope to examine the very delightful, "Completely Over Ted Turner, Let's Get On With It Jane Fonda 'Exercise Maneuvers' Regimen." This requires some flight training, regular 300-pound weight-lifting weights (bungee corded to the leg, a great thigh firmer), investments in an airfield, landing gear, helmet, and emergency flotation equipment, but it guarantees *forever firm upper arms!* (Available if instructions released by publicist.)

Till then—*Work that spine!*

5. Finances

Finances and the Middle-Aged Babe

One might wonder why we address "Finances" in this "Getting the Look" section of our guide to being a Middle-Aged Babe. In fact, ample finances are crucial for the Middle-Aged Babe to radiate attractiveness ("The Look") and well-being. As well, an attractive face and body, often acquired surgically, is costly (again, "finances"). But costly procedures may raise Babe spirits so she may achieve (give back) far more than if she looked like hell. Beauty radiates out *and* radiates in, likely motivating a Babe to spread her sense of well-being around and do good works. *Habitat for Humanity, The Red Cross,* and *Meals on Wheels* boast many artificially fluffed-up Babes (statistics not available). Regular, unfluffed Babes also do much for others, if motivated. And speaking of motivation—isn't it true—if you are up on a ladder, hammering a nail in the window of a two-bedroom home in Argentina, waving to a cute Argentine guy in the brush, you would rather appear attractive, as seen from below in your overalls, than not? Yes, good looks loosen the soul for good works. But ongoing beefing up of Babe Looks (and Moods!) requires a steady, reliable income (think of the cost of a mascara for a *Literacy Volunteers* lunch). Clearly, then, *everyone, worldwide,* benefits if the Babe wisely manages her finances, consistently improving her look, her well-being, and the look and well-being of the world at large.

Earning money counts. More important, INVESTING IT WELL! Many Babes have regrettably fallen behind in the investment aspect of their portfolio (if they have a portfolio). This world, with its ample granite countertops, is sadly, secretly, short of women with assets, investments, portfolios, even those little see-through banks shaped like pigs or the Liberty Bell, where you can see all the pennies but not get them out, even with a knife! Many in-the-closet nonsavers are now concerned or, more precisely, scared out of their drawers, about how, financially, they will proceed (with or without job/husband), improve their looks, give to others, retire, then die and leave things to people like hundred-dollar bills or even five-dollar bills! It is *that* population of Babes we now address.

Retirement

The Middle-Aged Babe must have some knowledge of finances, glaring, as she is, right into the headlights of retirement (if retirement may be thought to have headlights). Although retirement *is* a very distant time, *very* distant, *so* distant it is generally regarded, indeed defined, as, "That time, by which it arrives, we will have the money for it," this insane/correct way of perceiving it helps the Babe, but not so much as, say, a zillion dollars.

Some Babes Can Do Money

True, many Babes are hip to finance. Some are brokers themselves, showing they "understand," "know how to deal with," or "aren't petrified by" money. These babes do not have to read this and may skip instead to the section "How To Feng Shui Your Investments." For the others, the "less financially savvy" or "completely math/investment-impaired" Middle-Aged Babe, what follows is de rigueur.

Regardless of circumstance, all Middle-Aged Babes want to retire—and how does one do it unless one has a sound investment portfolio, a pension, or both, or a rich husband, rich parents, rich alimony settlement, Wimbledon championship purse, or a couple of Monets to sell or a string of huge black pearls you find on the ground on Fifty-seventh Street and Fifth Avenue, in a blue bag? Or more?

Secretly Poor Middle-Aged Babes

The "secretly poor" Middle-Aged Babe is a phenomenon of our appearance-driven society, where credit cards, granite counters, and faux Vuitton bags abound, but savings do not. These Babes (you know who you are) need a-little-late-in-the-day financial assistance: those with only ten, fifteen years till retirement must both lay, and hatch, a nest egg or else man the information counter at Barnes & Noble or the checkout at Krispy Kreme in perpetuity (the Krispy Kreme option clearly preferable but less so than a house in Tuscany). Or worse yet, what if you worked at the Krispy Kreme in Tuscany? And you rented there and everyone else owned? And you had to use the Tuscany Laundromat?

Panic Investing—Why It Works: Our Model Midlife Portfolio

The only route then, for the strapped-to-be Babe, is not simply "Speed Investing" (a term used by financial planners meaning: to accelerate investment return as retirement approaches) but "Panic Investing." This means setting aside maximum capital* in various "Panic Instruments" we will be disclosing here, some for the first time.

Our picks include little-known investments, chosen for maximum yet quick results, often quite "cutting-edge," for the requisite "Fast 'n' Fat return" the Krispy-Kreme-counter-bound Babe must enjoy. Our diversified "Panic Portfolio" is divided among the following:

Very little known, extremely aggressive stock and bond funds with exceptionally low initial investments ("no load") required, and the potential for unbelievably high, fast returns, as well as other new innovative speedy-return investment suggestions (listed by percentage of the portfolio). Nothing is written in stone: there are alternative suggested investments in many categories, such as new companies like "Bristol-Myers Squibb/Ebay" (auctioning off prescription drugs online, bought by those who don't need them but have insurance coverage, so fake symptoms and sell drugs to the uninsured—an exciting new way to control rising drug prices) *and* "Sprint PCS/State Farm Insurance" (a clear winner as cell phone use in cars increases, with its attendant dangers).

Here, then, our "A Little Late in the Day" investment guide:

The Middle-Aged Babe's "Panic Investment" Guide

Funds

8%—*The Prudential Short, Short Term Gaza Strip Municipal Bond Fund*—The goal of this fund is to see how long it can remain in business and to "capture" (and we do mean capture) high yields fast, in a unique no-load setting.

6%—*The Fidelity Mixed Multi-Size Cap Growth and Value, or Just Growth, or Maybe Just Value Fund*—A confused fund manager with a lot of kids to suddenly send to college isn't sure what he's going to do with this fund yet, so it's very cheap to get in. The fund will be either load or no-load, depending on the day you invest (and if any of the kids gets in early decision) and will involve, as the prospectus states, a lot of "really good companies or whatever." A mixed bag of high-tech, low-tech, and medium-tech investments, the fund will be a "fun" "semi-index maybe" fund that will combine the security of a money market with the volatility of the entire market! A no-load dream for the Bullish Babe, with real growth potential—*and surprises!!*

10%—*The Donna Karan Stretch Latex Waistband/Bodysuit-Growth Growth Fund*—Pegged to the aging arc of the Baby Boomers, this fund will invest mostly in Donna Karan designs made of stretch wool, or

---

* Money

wool/spandex, and certain evening dresses done in supple jersey latex, with or without sequins. Sleeveless styles will not be included.

8%—*The T. Rowe Price Lap Dance Misdemeanor Trust*—Capitalizes on the emerging lap dance phenomenon, with particular attention to the Orlando region.

10%—*The Oppenheimer Prozac, Aspertame, Inderal, Estrogen, and Craftmatic Bed Fund*—Again, tied to the aging arc of Boomers, this fund invests in companies responsive to American growth-market consumer sectors. (See also The Scudder Lipitor/IKEA /Kaiser Permanente Asset Allocation Trust and another Baby Boom "demise-driven fund": Putnam "Long-Term Care/Take with Food Global Assets.")

5%—*The Magellan Global Knocked Off Fifth Avenue, Status Logo Flea Market/Street Vendor Purse Fund*—Responsive to the Emerging Prada/Fendi/Gucci Flea Market/Street Fair Fakes Cartel, this fund assures very secure, "blue chip"–style gains over the long and short term, the main "value" instrument recommended.

6%—*The Artisan International Diversified Knocked Off Status Logo Flea Market Purse and Wallets Hedge Trust*—Much like the above, but this Value Trust incorporates the more lucrative "wallet" category (a less pricey, more liquid consumer item) and should be held as a hedge against the Magellan Fund (above), given its inclusion of Faux Louis Vuitton Luggage and Totes, as Faux LVMH products are seeing a greater and greater market share (note also The Scudder Small Leather-Like Goods Trust). (Held sumultaneously, these two funds shoud replicate the performance of the Standard and Poor's 500 Stock Index.)

2%—*The Vanguard Laetrile, Echinacea, Hot 'n' Sour Soup, Zinc, Ginkgo Biloba, Biotech Hedge Fund*—To counterweigh the risky med-tech sector, this fund capitalizes on exciting medical "Shadow Sector" investments. (See also "The Merrill Lynch Alpha Hydroxy/Retin-A/Injectable Cholesterol Derma-Plump Value Portfolio." This fund, the first to explore the likely upcoming miracle of "injectable cholesterol," to help replace depleted Botox mines in (as environmentalists warned) ravaged, newly depleted deposits in Africa.)

2%—*The Putnam Rogue Nations Short, Short Term Municipal Bond Fund* (self-explanatory)—(See also The Vanguard Short, Short, SHORT Term Worldwide Unstable-Figurehead-Government Bond Fund and The Vanguard Short Short Short Short Short Term Emerging Nuclear Armed Nations Global Growth or Global Total Destruction Fund—same fund manager.)

2%—*The Oppenheimer Sweet 'n' Low Future Class Action Suit Settlement Hedge Fund* (self-explanatory).

2%—*The Templeton Strategic McDonald's Promotional Toys/SpongeBob SquarePants Chuck E. Cheese Prizes/Swatch Watch/Possible Future Collectibles Equities Fund*—Rather than buy the collectibles themselves, this fund pools interests in companies that *create* collectibles, such that the possible value in the future of these merchandised products enhances the overall value of the companies that produce them. Thus, a potpourri of highly merchandised companies: the Walt Disney Company, McDonald's, Warner Bros., Burger King, the NFL, Cracker Jack, etc.

6%—*Lotto Tickets*—Divided equally (diversification is key with any investment) among "Pick Ten," "Instant Scratch-Off," "Easy Winner," "Bingo," with special attention to "$100,000 a Year for Life," and "Lucky Seven," these government-backed instruments provide a hedge against more so-called "statistically likely" but often volatile "broker's ideas."

10%—*Collectibles of the Future*—"Collectibles of the Future" are those items you need anyway (vacuum cleaners, toaster ovens, dishes from Target, shoes). Under this plan, you hold on to them forever in the garage, waiting for their "kitsch" value to increase. A "growth" or "slow growth" investment, but a great comfort when purchasing those "life necessities" that otherwise seem so "no-growth."

10%—*Emerging Growth Companies to Watch For*—Buying companies before projected mergers is always a smart investment strategy. Our suggestions of the best and the brightest:

- Boeing/Lancôme. Richly innovative in the field of moisturizing before landing, this joint venture promises rewards in interstellar cosmetology.
- IBM/Ronco (Ron Popeil). Technologically enhanced gizmos: The DOS-Pocket Fisherman, the Kitchen Magician with CD-ROM, etc.
- General Motors/General Mills/General Foods
- AOL-Time Warner/Oprah or Anything/Oprah
- Cingular/Hamburger Helper Instructions Box Panel Division
- FedEx/Tylenol 3

12%—*New Commodities*—"Futures Investing" (speculating on the rise or fall of upcoming prices for basics like pork bellies, frozen orange juice concentrate, and gold) is expanding. A few of our picks: "Greed," "Fat," "Synthetic Seratonin," "Over-the-Counter Dopamine," "Prescription Hairspray."

1%—*Cash*—Money you keep in the form of money, as in the perfectly titled "Money Market Fund." Examples include: "Certificates of Deposit (of money)," "Treasury Bills (paid back in money)," and the newer "Bottom of Your Purse Debentures" and "Fell Out of Your Pocket, Lying Under Your Car Seat, Tax-Free Annuities."

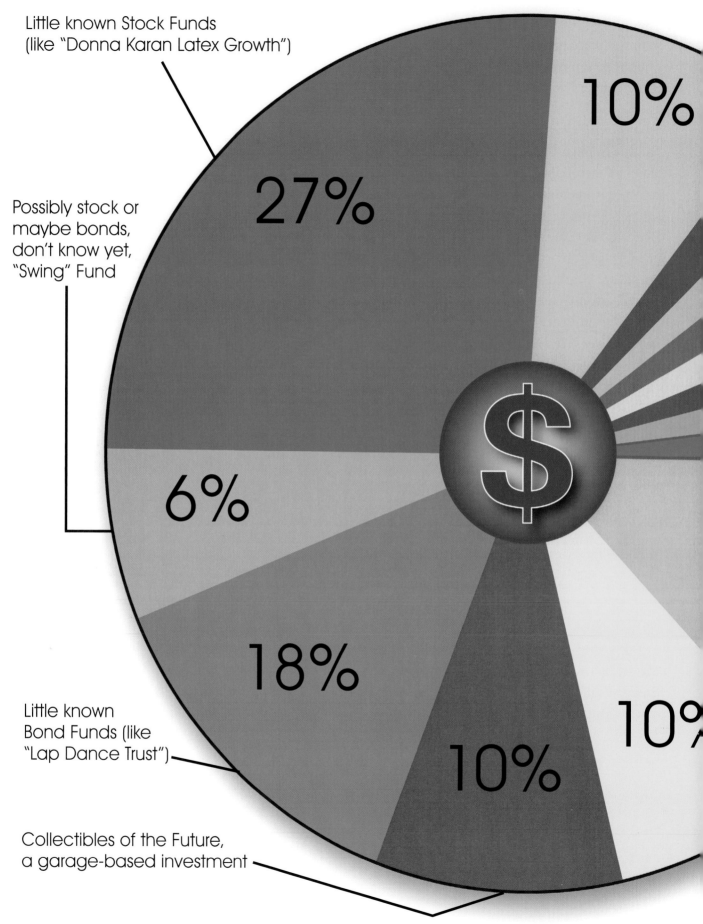

Little known Stock Funds
(like "Donna Karan Latex Growth")

10%

Possibly stock or
maybe bonds,
don't know yet,
"Swing" Fund

27%

6%

Little known
Bond Funds (like
"Lap Dance Trust")

18%

10%

10%

Collectibles of the Future,
a garage-based investment

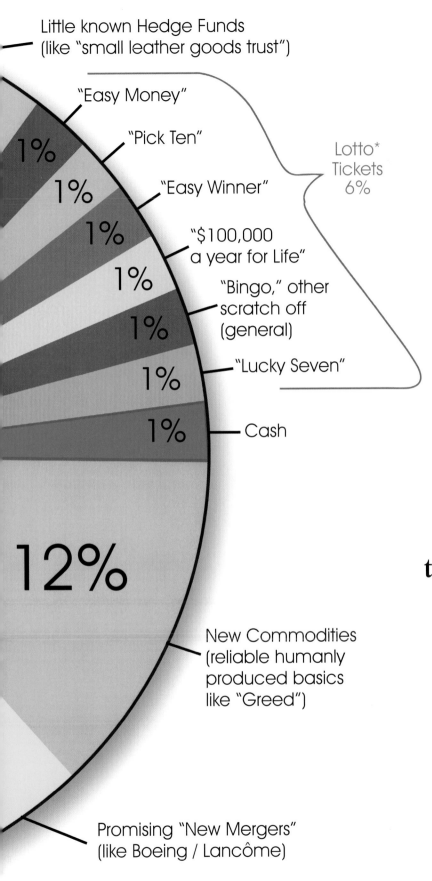

Little known Hedge Funds
(like "small leather goods trust")

1%

"Easy Money"

"Pick Ten"

1%

"Easy Winner"

1%

"$100,000
a year for Life"

1%

"Bingo," other
scratch off
(general)

1%

"Lucky Seven"

1%

Cash

1%

Lotto*
Tickets
6%

12%

New Commodities
(reliable humanly
produced basics
like "Greed")

Promising "New Mergers"
(like Boeing / Lancôme)

The
Middle-Aged
Babe's

"Only
Investment
Pie Chart
You'll Ever
Need Pie
Chart"

Our "A Little Late in
the Day" Buying Guide

* Savvy investors may also choose
"Winner Take All," "Set for Life," "Pot o'
Gold," and "Win $2000 a year for Life"
(pay particular attention to "Win $2000
a year for Life").

NOTE: Historically, Lotto has held its
own against Indian Reservation Bingo.

6. Beauty

Beauty and Age have always been strange bed-fellows, stranger still, with the advent of plastic surgery, causing them not even to recognize one another, yet to bed down together so eagerly, one could believe they might move in together, get married, and have children (if Age is a guy).* The "children" of Beauty and Age, of course, are orphans: they have no ancestors, no relatives, as never before in human history has "beauty" been a concept even faintly related to age. Now, with the ever-increasing age arc of Babehood, "Beauty" is available to anyone who can get out of bed (Age's bed) and take Perception in hand.

---

* Or maybe not such strange bedfellows, for, as the Middle-Aged Babe has learned: Where Beauty goes, Age inevitably will follow.

Age once could convince Beauty she was no longer viable. These days are laughable, moreover un-American—we, who zapped swinging Chicago from moribund prairie, conjured Texas from nothing, and willed Las Vegas from a desert; we, perennial "creators-from-zilch"—why shouldn't we induce "Beauty" from the one-time "Beast" of "Age"?

We can (within reason), and we will.

Actually, the Middle-Aged Babe *is,* on everyone's map, the exact *juncture* of Beauty and Age. Having agonized for decades over her appearance, the Middle-Aged Babe is ready to agonize more, only she'd prefer some mild, light agonizing. "Mild, light agony" is important to the Middle-Aged Babe, who has neither the strength nor disposition to ride herself for appearance's sake. Yes, she'll have a whole big surgical operation that will renovate her, but she will not, looking older, "beat *herself* up," as she knows a paid surgeon can do a far, far better job.

Later we will discuss wildly proliferating surgical (and chemical) Beauty Options for Middle-Aged Babes (and some delightful, new, budget-conscious Plastic Surgery You Can Do at Home). Here: non–Blue Cross improvements.

The Makeover

The makeover is a classic American form, like baseball and jazz, based on the ecstatic American notion that if you look wrong, someone can simply make you look right. Dorothy, entering the Emerald City, had a makeover (in *The Wizard of Oz*), as did Audrey Hepburn in *Funny Face,* and most notably, *Cinderella.* That, in fact, is the very *heart* of *Cinderella*: the mythic optimism of the makeover.

In fashion magazines, makeovers are done by celebrity makeup artists, "facial stylists" who sometimes write whole "how-to" books on them in which Cher always appears. "Facial Stylists" are often stars themselves and have big dramatic lives, flying here and there to do and undo faces bigger and better than your own, in private, "Facial Stylistic Equipped" jets. Money races, leaps into their checking accounts; their books have sequels, and the sequels have sequels. Yes, "Facial Stylists" have bigger, better lives than yours or anyone you might know or get to meet or even see. Glamorous lives you'd like to look like.

Makeovers are usually for young, whimsical, dopey, no-values, looks-obsessed people—things the Middle-Aged Babe isn't. Still, her *soul* must have "room" for the mythology of the concept. It is, after all, an excessively, even irrationally optimistic, hopeful idea: that a makeover can "transform" you. And what is a Middle-Aged Babe if not excessively, irrationally optimistic?

Thus, we present here the key to Outer Well-Being (which seeps inward), the Middle-Aged Babe Makeover (see *Psychology Today* or a good shrink for the sometimes appropriate "mental makeover").

Babe in a Minute: The Middle-Aged Babe One-Minute Makeover

"The makeover is the highest form of human self decorative cosmetic art," says Trey Eclat, facialist extraordinaire, our consulting beauty authority on the Middle-Aged Babe Makeover. Trey loves a makeover. "Taking an innocent person's face and ending up—after an Alpha Hydroxy probe, digging faux pores, creating an unconstructed mouth, lubing and widening the eye sockets—with someone so totally else . . .

that's timeless fashion," he says. "The Middle-Aged Babe's look should not be an 'in your face face' just fluffed up and pared down," Trey counsels. "Sadly," says Trey, "being human, you will never achieve the plastic mannequin-tight look of youth or, more regrettably, ever be a plastic mannequin. With celebs like Tashi Dashi, Electra D. Alisha, and Aliyasha beating down his Cessna door, and producing his own *Face Time* show on the Style network, clearly Trey's face passion is transporting to everyone.

As we talk, Trey, a wildly successful celebrity makeup artist, sits with business partner Junko Bressage, in the Soho studio/office of their company, "Cashbox," sipping his signature a.m. Kool-Aid—the office is decorated with his vast collection of fifties vintage Kool-Aid frosted pitchers with the faux-iced smiley faces, originals Trey as a kid sent away for, now has custom-made in his factory in Murano, Italy, keeping them in constant twenty-four-hour production, lest one break—as he struggles to identify what first inspired his "pared-down face" ethic. "It's so, so hard to pin down," he tells a visitor, stroking a vintage faux-iced smiley face Kool-Aid pitcher over and over.

Still, celebrities flock to his $5,000-a-session "facial rethinks." As we talk, he juggles Angelina on one line (who needs an "event face") and Reese on another (who wants "pulled-together brows"). Trey's look has engendered its own table at the *Vanity Fair* Oscar party, of facially pared-down celebs—all, once pared, *are pretty much virtually identical people, rifling place cards wildly to see what their own name is, as they can't tell each other apart!* (This is a coup for a facial manipulator who considers a person's individual features "a distraction.")

Trey has been a huge fan of Middle-Aged Babes since the eighties, when, struggling through Parsons School of Design, he lived (through the help of the doorman) in the porte-cochere of the River House (huddled in a cardboard refrigerator box, with his then signature look: used ski jacket, fuzzy Milk Duds in the pocket), sketching faces of wealthy, philandering matrons who, watching for private detectives, sprinted from their limos in the early a.m. (often, regrettably, stepping on him in his box). "They had pared-down aquiline noses and simple low heels that barely broke the skin," Trey reminisces. "The look was brilliant: "morning-after chic," which he considers perfect beauty, the totalness of "post-lovemaking, makeup-erasing simplicity."

That, he says, is his facial ethic *and* the optimum look for the Middle-Aged Babe, which she can achieve fast. "Time is the new black!" Trey laughs. "Everyone needs, wants, loves more time! Time is the new real estate," he says. "Time is the new love." Especially for the Middle-Aged Babe, time-pressed, for whom Trey has conceived the überquick "One-Minute Makeover." "To start the Middle-Aged Babe's One-Minute Makeover, we divide the face into four 'facial décor' quadrants"—eye, cheek, mouth, brow.

The One-Minute Eye

Trey says, "Life is seen through the face, and the soul is behind it; so when we do the eyes, we are adorning the portals of the soul, or 'soul holes.'" Important re: the eye? Enhancing color, opening it up with eye shadows that have a "translucent opaqueness."

To achieve, Trey first uses a "liquid powder" on the eye which self-selects the perfect skin shade, to bring out the eye when the light hits it. For lashes, Naturalist Trey uses a thin reed from a nearby wooded area, applying mascara with a "natural look." (See "easy-do"chart, next page.)

The One-Minute Eye

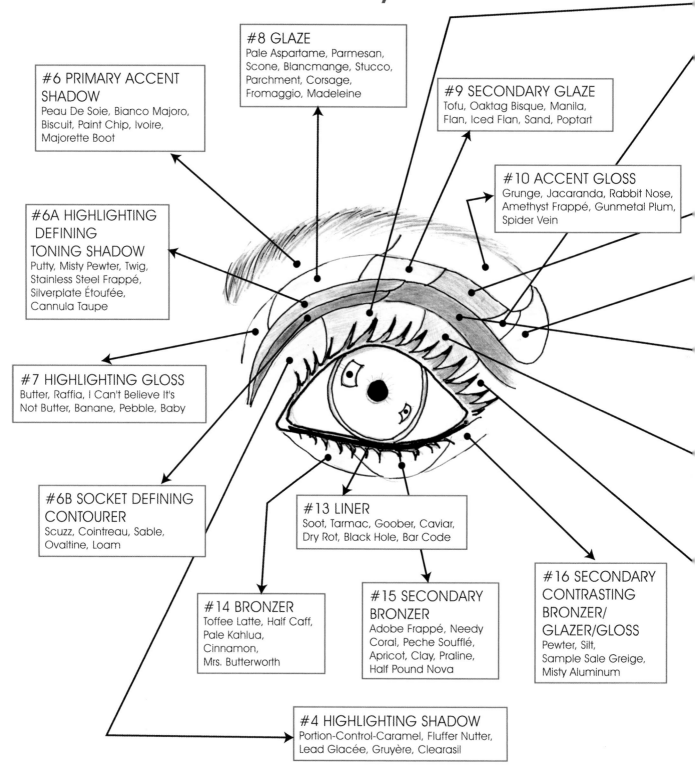

#8 GLAZE
Pale Aspartame, Parmesan, Scone, Blancmange, Stucco, Parchment, Corsage, Fromaggio, Madeleine

#6 PRIMARY ACCENT SHADOW
Peau De Soie, Bianco Majoro, Biscuit, Paint Chip, Ivoire, Majorette Boot

#9 SECONDARY GLAZE
Tofu, Oaktag Bisque, Manila, Flan, Iced Flan, Sand, Poptart

#10 ACCENT GLOSS
Grunge, Jacaranda, Rabbit Nose, Amethyst Frappé, Gunmetal Plum, Spider Vein

#6A HIGHLIGHTING DEFINING TONING SHADOW
Putty, Misty Pewter, Twig, Stainless Steel Frappé, Silverplate Étoufée, Cannula Taupe

#7 HIGHLIGHTING GLOSS
Butter, Raffia, I Can't Believe It's Not Butter, Banane, Pebble, Baby

#6B SOCKET DEFINING CONTOURER
Scuzz, Cointreau, Sable, Ovaltine, Loam

#13 LINER
Soot, Tarmac, Goober, Caviar, Dry Rot, Black Hole, Bar Code

#16 SECONDARY CONTRASTING BRONZER/ GLAZER/GLOSS
Pewter, Silt, Sample Sale Greige, Misty Aluminum

#14 BRONZER
Toffee Latte, Half Caff, Pale Kahlua, Cinnamon, Mrs. Butterworth

#15 SECONDARY BRONZER
Adobe Frappé, Needy Coral, Peche Soufflé, Apricot, Clay, Praline, Half Pound Nova

#4 HIGHLIGHTING SHADOW
Portion-Control-Caramel, Fluffer Nutter, Lead Glacée, Gruyère, Clearasil

#1 SHADOW
Beauty Myth Pink, Pale Raspberry Rose, Bolognese Au Creme, Ballerina Mousse, Cherry Sorbet, Wan Plum, Pale Cerise, Aspergum, Quartz Au Lait, Blanche Magenta, Au Jus, Ventricle Rose

#12 ACCENT SHADOW
Tutu, Puff, Toedance, Twinkie, Booboo, Charmin, Girl Pink

#11 CONTOURING ACCENT
Light White, Dark White, Aspercreme, Creme Fraiche Au Lait, Chiclet, Brie, Glacé, Tuxedo Shirt, Igloo, Cool Whip, Ranch, Mikimoto

#5 CONTOURING HIGHLIGHTER
Dark/Dark Brown, Medium Dark Brown, Algae, Sushi, Timber, Ash, Spore, Melanoma, Drunk Mayan, Canyon

#2 SECONDARY SHADOW
Gunmetal Pink, Mochalata, Tartare, Mauve Pearlescence, Cranberry Bud Lite, Aubergine Almondine

#3 SECOND SECONDARY SHADOW
Mauve/Taupe, Pale Grunge, Tabac Soufflé, Terrazzo Mist

While advocating "speedy chic" and "slapdash dash," makeup magician Trey cautions the Middle-Aged Babe to be an "honor guard in the 'sallow patrol': never use a shade that is too too awful!" How? Match skin tone to foolproof "celeb color icons" (which Junko himself (a full partner) proudly thought up after a brief tussle about publishing rights and who really did what on East Hampton Beach). "Ask yourself," Junko advises, as it is all his idea, all of it, every last bit. Are you a "Rose/Beige" like Jimmy Carter, a "Grey/Beige" like Dwight Eisenhower, a "Dark Grey/Beige" like Louis Armstrong, a "Summer Citrus" like Madeleine Albright, or a "White/White" like Dannon Vanilla Yogurt? "Each shade in my line works for certain skin types," sighs Trey resentfully, handing Junko a huge check. "Just find your matching celeb skin icon on these shade selection charts." Junko's advice to color tone junkies: tear out celebs for color-easy match-ups anywhere. ("I've taken Louis Armstrong to Saks, Costco, and the Bahamas!" jokes Junko. "See what looks good with him! He's genius at point-of-purchase!")

Rose/Beige

Grey/Beige

Dark Grey/Beige

Summer Citrus

White/White

You can wear . . .			If you're a . . .		
Ballerina Mousse	Dark Grey/Beige	Rose/Beige	Grey/Beige	White/White	Summer Citrus
Aspergum	Dark Grey/Beige	Rose/Beige	NO	NO	NO
Ventricle Rose	NO	NO	Grey/Beige	White/White	Summer Citrus
Tutu	NO	Rose/Beige	NO	NO	NO
Girl Pink	NO	NO	NO	NO	Summer Citrus
Light White	Dark Grey/Beige	Rose/Beige	Grey/Beige	NO	NO
Majorette Boot	Dark Grey/Beige	Rose/Beige	Grey/Beige	White/White	Summer Citrus
Pale Aspartame	NO	Rose/Beige	Grey/Beige	White/White	Summer Citrus
Oaktag Bisque	Dark Grey/Beige	NO	NO	NO	Summer Citrus

The One-Minute Eye

You can wear . . .	If you're a . . .				
Misty Aluminum				NO	NO
Lead Glacé					
Clearasil				NO	NO
Scuzz	NO	NO			
Ovaltine	NO		NO		NO
Loam				NO	
Amethyst Frappé					
Gunmetal Plum			NO	NO	NO
Spider Vein	NO	NO			
Tarmac	NO		NO		NO
Dry Rot					
Black Hole					
Sample Sale Greige			NO		NO
I Can't Believe It's Not Butter	NO	NO			
Baby		NO	NO		NO
Needy Coral	NO	NO		NO	
Half Pound Nova				NO	NO
Paint Chip					
Blancmange	NO				
Corsage		NO	NO	NO	
Fromaggio					
Madeleine			NO	NO	NO
Grunge	NO				
Gunmetal Plum	NO		NO		NO
Peche Soufflé	NO	NO	NO	NO	
Pale Kahlua				NO	NO
Rabbit Nose					
Portion-Control-Caramel					
Fluffer Nutter	NO	NO	NO	NO	

The One-Minute Cheek

Trey now moves to "the needy cheek, with 'me, me, me' pores," he says. "All skin is needy, always saying "feed me, touch me, caress me, hydrate me, don't walk into clouds of car exhaust in me, don't take me to movies with subtitles," and on and on and on. You may think your skin is all about you, but to skin, it's all about it."

Prefoundation, Trey applies sluffing lotion, low-high-maintenance masque, nose refresher, citrus toner, then orders a geological survey to determine the "peaks and valleys of the facial dermal landscape." He often inserts small flags on toothpicks into the face, marking elevations, to contour it. He highlights cheekbones, shades nose, elevates the jaw, and creates "facial topography." Then, foundation in a color-correcting hue. "We are all a color, but we all need to be corrected," quips Trey. "It gives a woman the fabulous look of overall skin." Finally, Trey applies a "volumizing face detangler," his own "Cashbox" fave, demi-blush, to get the "no-look look" he's famous for.

The One-Minute Cheek

Trey's Tips

"Try to use a white that is the white of your eyeball. Otherwise, coordinate with teeth or bones."

"Pull the cheekbone taut, then apply highlighter."

"Sculpt face by encouraging cheeks to hollow out, either by stern talking or reprimands."

"Use skin-colored skin makeup."

"Elevate face by using blond blusher."

"Follow with all-over color in your racial tonality."

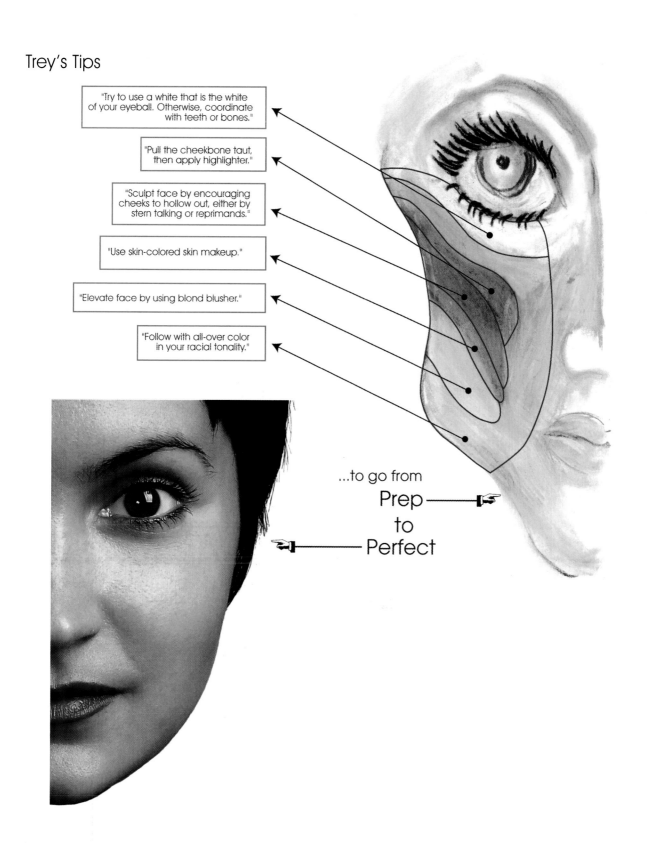

...to go from
Prep
to
Perfect

The One-Minute Mouth

Trey loves a strong cheek and lip look. He starts with a tightening egg white "lip-masque" stroked on lips with a pastry brush, then uses a vitamin E pearly opalescent mouth balm, after a vigorous "lip pore scrub." Now the "naturalized" lip is ready for color, but which? Trey's "perfect color find" trick—"Hold your tongue between your teeth, then match lip color to tongue color. Leave tongue in this position to color-code lip liner, which should be two shades darker than your tongue." After lip gloss, "Fluff with powder, as lip gloss feathers, writhes, and often climbs right off the face," Trey advises. (See Trey's color-coded lip shade selections below.)

The One-Minute Mouth

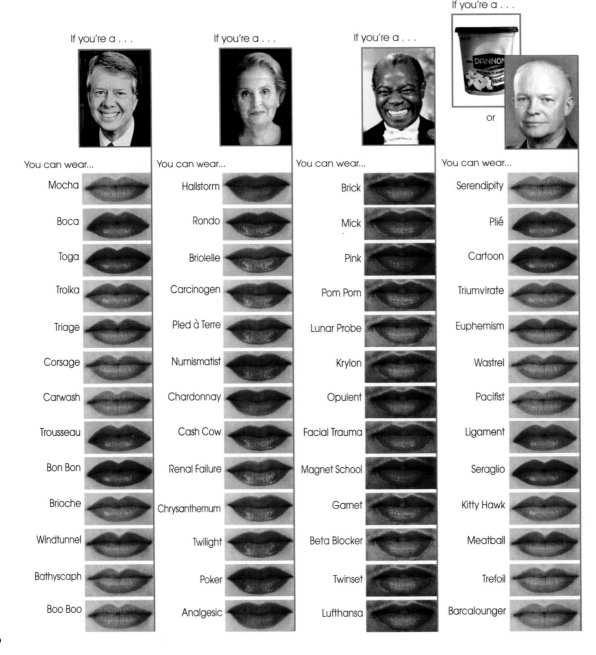

If you're a . . .	If you're a . . .	If you're a . . .	If you're a . . . or
You can wear...	You can wear...	You can wear...	You can wear...
Mocha	Hailstorm	Brick	Serendipity
Boca	Rondo	Mick	Plié
Toga	Briolelle	Pink	Cartoon
Troika	Carcinogen	Pom Pom	Triumvirate
Triage	Pied à Terre	Lunar Probe	Euphemism
Corsage	Numismatist	Krylon	Wastrel
Carwash	Chardonnay	Opulent	Pacifist
Trousseau	Cash Cow	Facial Trauma	Ligament
Bon Bon	Renal Failure	Magnet School	Seraglio
Brioche	Chrysanthemum	Garnet	Kitty Hawk
Windtunnel	Twilight	Beta Blocker	Meatball
Bathyscaph	Poker	Twinset	Trefoil
Boo Boo	Analgesic	Lufthansa	Barcalounger

The One-Minute Brow

The Babe has but a minute to ready her face for public use. Simplify daily brow-shaping by cutting out preferred "brow hut." Pop out preferred brow shape, place over existing brow (flip to backside for right), and color in with appropriate brow pencil. Don't let paper crunch or bunch up, shred, or get wet with tears of frustration. What could be easier?

"Eyebrow Hut" stencil cards

The Sarah Jessica Parker "Way Downtown" Eyebrow

The Jane Wyman "Rose Covered Cottage/Forties Film Version of Life" Eyebrow

The Frida Kahlo "Fab Latin American Art Gal" Eyebrow

The Cleopatra "Liz Taylor Arch" Eyebrow

The Lauren Hutton "Hormone Replacement Therapy, Cool Down" Eyebrow

The Laura Bush "Good Sport and Grooming Even in a Quonset Hut" Eyebrow

cut on dotted line   57

A Seminal Moment in Brow History

Shown here, as hung on Trey's Paris walls, original "Eyebrow huts," from which clients could choose their brow arch. First, of course, the "Frida Kahlo Brow," a wild, South American look. Below, the "Liz Taylor Brow," a Cleopatra arch. Hut pictures found in Paris flea market.

The Frida Kahlo "Fab Latin American Art Gal" Eyebrow

The Cleopatra "Liz Taylor Arch" Eyebrow

The Lauren Hutton "Hormone Replacement Therapy, Cool Down" Eyebrow

The Jane Wyman "Rose Covered Cottage/Forties Film Version of Life" Eyebrow

7. Plastic Surgery

History chronicles man's penchant for morphing into the Attractive Other. The wicked "Mirror, Mirror on the Wall" queen,* the frog who turned into a prince, the pre-pumpkin Cinderella—all major historical figures who presaged today's "anatomical teardown," insta-bod plastic surgery.

To arrive in Middle Age exactly when anatomies are disposable is a Babe timing perk. Buttocks and faces (equals at last) may put decades on "rewind" (one pulled up, the other down, then removed, cut, stitched). How Betsy Ross would have *qvelled* at today's plastic surgeon's "human needlework." The best: work not perceived, upstaged by new hair color, tinted contacts, or "seeming drunk."

The "red carpet ready face," desirable as it is secret, is uniformly hungered for: nobody doesn't want plastic surgery anymore (even men) and nobody can't not have it (demand grows, costs decline). So Babes who start as Sylvia Miles can enjoy a "Meg Ryan" result. It's fast—post-swelling, bruising, oozing, and drain removal—it's Super-Sized "Take-Out Beauty."

---

* See Appendix AA for "A Child's Treasury of Best-Loved Plastic Surgery: Highlights from the Wicked Queen in Snow White to the Frog Prince in The Frog Prince," for a complete historical overview of children's literature, and its presaging of both adult overhauls and desirable kid "big bucks medical careers."

Further Benefits: Outer Babe Begets Inner Babe

Waiting for her procedure on line outside Manhattan Eye, Ear and Throat Hospital, the reticent Babe should recall the ambient effects of her procedure: as she's enhanced so she perks up within, may even cheer up passersby. And long-standing enemies! Great beauty is "projectile beauty," elating the Babe, her Man, friends, family, and whole voting precinct.

Frequent questions:

Movie Stars Look Great, Yet They Say They've Had No Work. True?

This is the largest living lie in the Western Hemisphere, insisted on so when films are seen, audiences ignore plot, character, dialogue, and performance, preferring to intently search performers' eyes, cheeks, and jawlines for telltale "revisions." Such stars imperceptibly tweak their whole body (via surgeons), then credit, on talk shows, their centuries of unchanged good looks to diet and exercise. Lie. Such majorly overscheduled people, in fact, are having things done all the time, *probably even while they're saying they're not on TV* (through some faux wall, part of the talk show set, mobile plastic surgery teams are probably discreetly lifting a lid *while* the Star decries such barbaric procedures on the air). Stars are "serviced on the go": special limos equipped with plastic surgical "mobile units" can remove ribs en route to Nobu, assuring nipped-in waists post-dinner. However, "ongoing rib removal" and its resultant "upper body absence" suggest conscientious abstaining. Still, procedures go where celebs go: to costume fittings, where, on site, noses are shaved down to slide into too tight turtlenecks. For English period films, wrists, necks, and collarbones are preshrunk, chiseled, and chamois-shined, to bring out a kind of "pearlescence" typical of the Age, making them "period delicate," engendering a wan look and swanlike bones. Lesser-known "basted, pleated abs," "whipstitched Hadassah arms," and "donor behinds" (often temporary, using Novocain and sharp handstitch needles) won't replace "pec implants" and "instep heightening" (wherein the arch is broken and reset "up," to accommodate ever higher stilettos). Still: bye-bye Body Doubles. The Middle-Aged Babe's lucky to be alive now!

What Procedures Might a Babe Choose?

For the active Babe, "load-bearing" changes benefit looks, performance. "Stretch mark rescinding," "rear end addendum hike-ups," and "bikini-overall-look-overhauls" are most common for the General Babe, the sort of "Banana Republic Ready" procedures that can casually outfit her for life.

And for skin, before Botox or painful Chemical Peels, consider "skin outsourcing," done by plastic surgeons who "shop the body's map," move "less used patches" (e.g., the back) to overused sites (imagine!). Consider.

And How Do I Afford It?

Cost, dashed over earlier, ignores the burgeoning "Plastic Surgery Bubble" some economists predict. Due to hyperdemand and limited local practitioners, prices in some regions keep rising with no end in sight (as your stomach once did). Knowing her stomach is capable of so ignoble a look, the Babe will want to splash down any ready cash while procedures are still affordable. Hedge with equally priced shares of Clinique, Revlon, and Lancôme, should a plastic surgery crash eventually devalue your "new nose."

What About Effects on My Life Partner: How Will He Feel When I Become a Younger, Svelter, Virtually Unrecognizable Version of Me?

Great.

How Do I Pick a Surgeon?

The Babe goes to the guy who thinks she doesn't need surgery. He likes your look but with prodding will reluctantly "refine" it. Still, he'll like it while he's cutting and will create a "better, updated, final draft" of *you!*

No, But Really, How Can I Afford It?

The real question: How can you not? To pay, *simply move cash from your ATM directly into your doctor's pocket, in the amount he designates.* Alternatively, return things you bought within the year, sans receipt, just your American Express *bill:* this will net some bucks. Pricey stores take back rags without tags worn endlessly (shop there) if you have sales slips! Keep! (Plan well in advance to finance this.) Yard sales or "fake estate sales" (well advertised), where the "deceased" (you) sells everything she (you) "owned." (*Bonus:* You get to see how stuff you've worn really looks, as strangers try all your clothes on.) One Babe put her breast reduction on MediCal. Get online and *learn how!* Find medical deficits in your derriere (lower-back pain), thighs (lower-back pain), or abs (see previous); invent medical causes, reasons for, say, a tummy tuck. Read the PDR and let your imagination fly!!

Do I Really Need a Doctor?

This question, considered for centuries (barbers pulled tonsils), is particularly salient for today's college-tuition-hemorrhaging, retirement-nearing, "Funds-Lite" Babe. There's an answer we've withheld—a delightful, simple alternative:

Plastic Surgery You Can Do at Home*

As "facial upgrades" and "body tweaks" have cultural acceptance everywhere, from the mosh pit to the Kennedy Center Lifetime Achievement Awards, one realizes: Martha Stewart went to prison, forced felons to do aerobics, made them size 8s when they were all 24Ws, but how? Willpower and drive, matched only by the Babe's. Money need not discourage a full-bod Babe overhaul. *Extreme Makeover,* The House and Garden Channel, and Home Depot have generated ideas herein. Thus the Babe, gifted with a glue gun even when using it on herself, becomes her own "Go To" expert for a lovely, invasive, at-home overhaul!

---

* Be sure to get your doctor's approval before performing any plastic surgical procedures at home described in this book, in any book, or, God forbid, devised in your own mind.

Liposuction You Can Do at Home

What You Will Need

1. Garden hose (length sufficient to become the size you want—8 feet for sizes 4 to 6; 10 feet for sizes 8 to 10; 12 feet for sizes 10 to 12; 40 feet for size 12 and up)

2. Several old empty gasoline cans, or Sam's Club–size peanut butter jars, cleaned thoroughly

3. Funnel: the kind used to siphon gas in a film noir movie with Edward G. Robinson. Describe it this way to the sales associate at Home Depot.

4. A syringe, "borrowed" from your dentist's office after a "checkup," and a little "borrowed lidocaine," which you can drop in your purse. Alternatively, for the syringe: check local playgrounds or inner cities coast to coast; just walk around and look down.

5. Airline tubing—transparent plastic tubes from aquarium stores (provide bubbles "invisibly" from behind rocks, etc.), for use as insert to garden hose, or with syringes drugstores hand out free to give babies medications. These can be used on small spots, slipped in evening bags for spur-of-the-moment "lipo touch-ups" in ladies' rooms after, for example, noting how shatteringly thin everyone else at dinner is but you.

6. An eyedropper, into the bottom of which has been inserted a sewing machine needle, sterilized

7. Duct tape

8. Large three-way mirror

9. Two or three vacuum cleaners (we prefer bagless)

10. Bactine

How to Make a Cannula

This is that thing they insert that moves all around in you and sucks fat. Go to a party store, buy party blower noisemakers. Rip off noisemaker part, insert bottom cardboard part into garden hose, wrap with duct tape, insert opposite end into vacuum cleaner, turn switch to "On" and voilà!

How to "Score" "Anesthesia" on the "Street"

"The street," of course, is anywhere in a city that's paved; "anesthesia" is available from a variety of "dealers" from whom one may "cop" (purchase) useful premedicating drugs. One won't know *which* drug one is buying, even if one is "told," but isn't that half the fun? Also, both the "patient" and "doctor" will be medicated (possibly often the case in hospitals). If you're weirded out, go steal from your dentist again.

How to "Lipo" You!

OK, lots and lots of shots of whatever, then the Brave Babe makes an eensy, weensy puncture wound with the sterile Sewing Machine/Eyedropper/Liposuction Puncture tool. Insert the "Party Blower Cannula," flick on the vacuum, and suck out excess self to desired size. Apply Bactine.

Which Is the Fat?

I think it's the yellow or white stuff. If it's any other color, leave it there (in your body) or, if you've already taken it out, put it back.

How Will I Feel and for How Long?

Depending on the part of the body you've selected, you'll either ache wildly for months, such that you'll never sleep, or ache slightly for weeks, so that you'll never sleep. Establish a Pain Management Problem PRE-SURGERY with a reputable doctor (limping, demanding an MRI on some quote-unquote "painful area"), and get the doctor to write you a script for Percocet till a diagnosis can be made. (This fellow is also a handy "back-burner-MD" in case of spurting, hemorrhaging, or any other medical dilemma after your special secret home "human crafts" project.

Can I Do My Own Breast Enlargement at Home?

Yes, but this involves elves to build scaffolding (they take days and days and are notoriously poor workers), wearing 3-D glasses throughout the procedure to achieve proper imagined size and balance, and numerous complex moves involving a hot glue gun and pinking shears, *and* creating a Minwax-colored, free-standing, kiln-fired nipple and aureola, something a beginner may decline to attempt.

The Face Lift You Can Do at Home

The wise, economical Babe, unable to prod a young new plastic surgeon in a Marriott bar into becoming his own living, breathing local ad, gratis (as he starts his practice in town), may have to do her own face-lift at home. "Self-lifts" are hardly beyond the fiercely driven Babe but are admittedly trend-setting, on the level, say, of a Home Space Shuttle Launch.

What You Will Need
1. Three-way standing mirror (from Wal-Mart or JCPenney catalogue)
2. Embroidery hoop
3. Good sewing scissors
4. 100 boiled and sterilized Bic pen plastic insides, emptied of ink and Scotch-taped together in groups of five (to act as "drains" in the back of the head: yes, it sounds ooky, but not to the motivated Babe!)
5. Dritz number 10 embroidery needle
6. Staple gun (get the guy at Home Depot to help select)

How to Do a Face Lift at Home

1. Regretfully, more dental work must be "needed," as you must "borrow" another syringe and lidocaine from your dentist. Maybe just go for a cleaning. Sorry.
2. Put itsy-bitsy injections of lidocaine around hairline, chin, and behind ears. Ouch, but keep thinking how great Goldie Hawn looks, and how long she's looked that way.
3. Take pair of sewing scissors (good ones, well sharpened, don't skimp on necessities!). Cut off your face.*

---

* Do this standing center in the three-way mirror, on a Hefty Bag—not fun, but again, think Goldie, Meg, Barbra, and so many, many others, having laugh-filled, face-lifted lives that are, in some way the Middle-Aged Babe doesn't yet know, so much better than her own! Think of that as many times as necessary.

4. Drape your face over embroidery hoop. Snip off 1/2 inch per decade you wish to lose (up to three decades).

5. Replace your face on your body's "face place." Looking in mirror, use boiled Dritz number 10 embroidery needle to "whipstitch" former face back on, being careful to baste in Bic pen drains behind ears. Wow—almost done!

Think Goldie!

Exterior Stapling How-To's

1. Gently staple remainder of face (with Bic pen drains on back of head) back on, avoiding hair! (Get electric staple gun.) Rest up a little, have graham crackers and Percocet. If you can walk, walk (and the motivated Middle-Aged Babe certainly can!), have a diet soda and think of how giving up that trip to Costa Rica during your week off, to stay home instead and cut off your own face, was not so bad, as now you'll look as rested as if you went to Costa Rica (after the black, blue, yellow, purple, and green bruises go away). What a vacation!

2. Feeling woozy? Longer than 20 minutes? The savvy Middle-Aged Babe knows: call an ambulance and check into Mt. Sinai (there are Mt. Sinais everywhere). Take note of hunky ambulance driver; check his left hand for ring if conscious. Remember—*inpatient means no cooking!*

Alternatives to Home Plastic Surgery: The "Party Chat Arch" and the "Interactive Arch"

The Party Chat Arch (a joint design inspired by renowned plastic surgeon Dr. Sherrell Aston and an innovative carpenter) appears to others as an architectural detail of your living room but is built (see plans in Appendix E) by you at home and set up in the living room, with you under it, right before a party. It is lined in back with acoustic guitar string "tuners" (those plastic knobs on guitars around which guitar wire is wound, shortened or lengthened to get the precise key). Here, the see-through guitar string is attached to various sagging, drooping spots on you, hoists up everything (arm flab, jowls, cheek droop) before guests arrive, so you can chat all night, *standing under the arch*, looking fabulous, only you can't walk, run, turn, bend, sit, or go to the bathroom. The Interactive Arch, however, is hinged (permitting sitting, driving, reading a book in bed, even having easygoing sex with your partner, so long as the guitar strings don't "pop," zinging the Babe or her brave lover).

So Plastic Surgery's a "Babe Requirement"?

No. But looking good engenders feeling good. Which is good. This simple truth drives millions of patients into the arms of admitting personnel at hospitals worldwide. And if you're saving for retirement (and choose the At Home Alternative), you can even do At Home Implants: wad up a tennis sock and use a Ping-Pong ball, Dr. Scholl's bunion pad, or other inert, nonbiodegradable thing to make chin, cheekbones, or other regions more prominent. Break off the handle of a Tupperware scoop and voilà . . . new chin!

Soon. Plastic surgery rarely becomes a compulsion for someone unless everything becomes a compulsion for them. Clearly, though, it can require a great, great many elves, and it hurts. A governing principle, gleaned by observing hundreds of celebrities' out-of-control repeat plastic surgery, is: the Babe must choose her "moments." Liposuction (from the Latin, *Lipitos,* which means "sucks") is comprised of the word "Lip," the fattest part of the face, and the word "Osuction," Welsh for "once every seven years and probably not even then." This provides a guiding principle: repeat surgery may be performed, as a rule, only after birthdays with a seven in them. One exception: plastic surgery must occur prior to all class reunions.

Plastic Surgery Conclusions

The Middle-Aged Babe is beautiful inside, which oozes outside. She gives off the unmistakable musk of self-assuredness, sensuality, and other similar words. Her beauty is in her soul. But she acknowledges: time not only passes, it ravages; and she may yearn for physical enhancement. She may also choose to do nothing and "just be" (depending on her mood and how many clothes still fit). (Still, observing cohorts go through repeat surgical procedures, who actually bloom with heightened youth through the years, a strange inverse bodily reaction to the passage of time, may "piss off" the Nonsurgically Inclined Babe, as her look has traveled in the opposite direction.) Babes of all ages and all eras like "pretty" (the attractive childhood tinsel in the hair at Christmas, or bow on the nose on one's third birthday). They likely view plastic surgery as a viable alternative to the once superhot look (old and fat), all the rage in pre-pogrom Europe. Plastic surgery may be for the Babe; it may not. We leave her face to her.*

In Appendix F we address the too-thin Babe, discuss Donor Fat, "How to Get on a Donor Fat Registry," and (coming soon) Raloxitox, that fabulous new combination of Raloxifene and Botox, injected into the face as a hot flash deflector/wrinkle buster in one! For the Less Medically Rambunctious Babe, we direct you back to "The One-Minute Makeover" and "Compensatory Underwear."

---

* Re: historically natural beautification drive, see "From Urchin to Goddess and Back: Mythology of Beauty as Life Source, a Study of Women and Crudely Inflicted, Archaeologically Unearthed Failed Plastic Surgery Through the Ages," from *The Incurable Archaeologist,* Issue One of One, Princeton Library, storage center, under the air-conditioning housing, basement.

8. Sex: You've Got Male
The Middle-Aged Babe's Complete Guide to Men

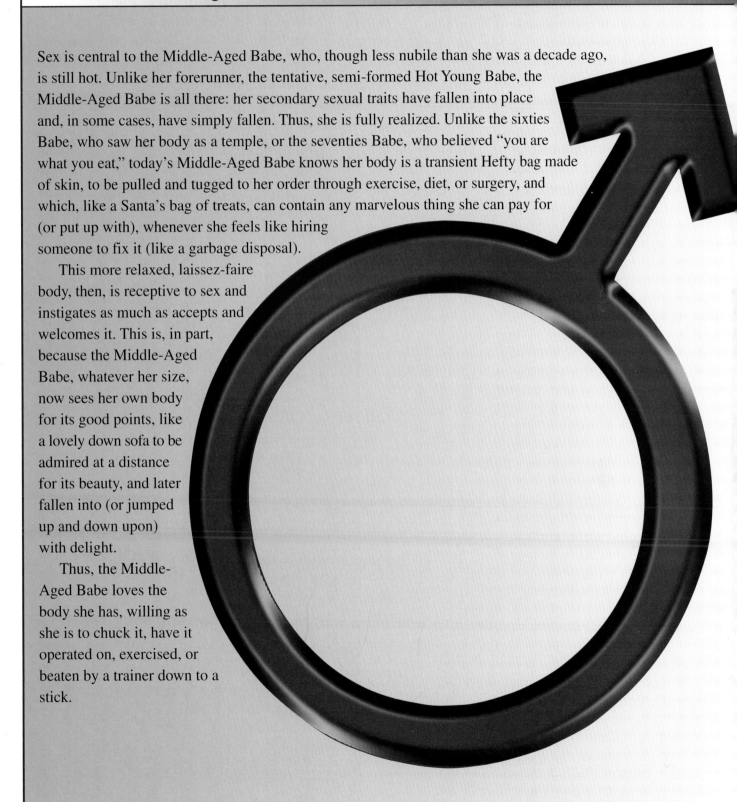

Sex is central to the Middle-Aged Babe, who, though less nubile than she was a decade ago, is still hot. Unlike her forerunner, the tentative, semi-formed Hot Young Babe, the Middle-Aged Babe is all there: her secondary sexual traits have fallen into place and, in some cases, have simply fallen. Thus, she is fully realized. Unlike the sixties Babe, who saw her body as a temple, or the seventies Babe, who believed "you are what you eat," today's Middle-Aged Babe knows her body is a transient Hefty bag made of skin, to be pulled and tugged to her order through exercise, diet, or surgery, and which, like a Santa's bag of treats, can contain any marvelous thing she can pay for (or put up with), whenever she feels like hiring someone to fix it (like a garbage disposal).

This more relaxed, laissez-faire body, then, is receptive to sex and instigates as much as accepts and welcomes it. This is, in part, because the Middle-Aged Babe, whatever her size, now sees her own body for its good points, like a lovely down sofa to be admired at a distance for its beauty, and later fallen into (or jumped up and down upon) with delight.

Thus, the Middle-Aged Babe loves the body she has, willing as she is to chuck it, have it operated on, exercised, or beaten by a trainer down to a stick.

Current Dismay

As to sex—the Middle-Aged Babe is dismayed by the apparent lack of sexiness sex is portrayed with on TV and in magazines. Shows like *Sex and the City* and *Desperate Housewives* have included a great variety and amount of sex (to their credit) but without evoking sex as something, well, dirty.

Instead, the various sex acts on view seem offhand, societally de rigueur, and boringly abundantly discussed. Today's matter-of-fact, TV tabloid sex seems too public to the Middle-Aged Babe, for when one's heart (or vulva) is on one's sleeve, it loses its essence of privileged, private evocativeness.

In a recent fashion magazine, a woman describes a Brazilian bikini wax, which includes *having her labia waxed, then showing it to fellow office workers after lunch.* This, though not a sex act itself, allows the magazine to print the words "waxed labia" and "labia wax" as "faux sex mentions," and indicates perhaps real sex, the actual act, has taken a hit in the culture and is falling to lower and lower numbers of performances, like vaudeville at the end of vaudeville. The writer on the hair-free labia admits her sex life is nil (*this,* apparently, the new titillating reveal). The Babe, ever hot, misses the old deep, full-bodied fashion magazine and network TV sex *silence!*

Sex, it appears, is now being had principally in the form of a labia wax, or enacted by surrogates—TV actors, diluting Real Sex for everyone else.

Romance/Sex

Romance is central to the Middle-Aged Babe, whose soul is nourished through the love of a good man, or even a semi-good one, as necessity dictates, and by loving such a man back.

But the Middle-Aged Babe's sexual history is the most complicated sexual history in history due to the era in which she "came to bloom." Thus, the Middle-Aged Babe comes in a variety of "romance formats": married late, married early, divorced, never divorced, never married, serial marriage, serial divorce, and/or (God forbid) living together. Never before have there been such multiformatted women.*

The Middle-Aged Babe, then, brings to any new relationship a lot of "emotional baggage" or, to defuse and slightly feminize this phenomenon, let us say "emotional baguettes," which may cause small difficulties in upcoming relationships with men. Certain "heavy" or "diamond" baguettes may counterbalance her relationship difficulties.

Ways to Outwit a Babe's Own Mental State

Such a Babe must outfox her own mental state. When it comes to new men, the Middle-Aged Babe doesn't need lower expectations but newer expectations, as this New Life Stage suggests. True, we are temporal creatures, basing our expectations on past experience, but for the particularly bitter Babe, throwing out past expectations and replacing them with "fond backward glances at marvelous events that have not ever yet happened, but could quite possibly occur and can be imagined" is ideal.

---

* And, like certain taping devices that have had many formats (beta, eight-track, reel-to-reel), the Middle-Aged Babe may have been reformatted one too many times and may break or require extensive servicing. This sensitivity should be kept in mind, by her and those fucking around with her.

Loving Looks Back at the Future

Such "loving looks back at the future" or "happy forward memories" may help steady the badly format-ted Babe, enabling her to commence a new romance without "emotional baguettes," "diamond baguettes," and without trashing it before it even begins (a sad trait of the poorly formatted Babe, whose "love history" makes her, quite frankly, a soupçon insane). Is it not less insane, then, if this Babe looks back fondly on fabulous things she has only just now dreamed up and prays will happen, even repeat, though they never occurred in the first place? This happy fact is the wise Babe's sole defense in our cur-rent romance-strafed, love-battered, emotionally dehydrated universe.

And the Middle-Aged Babe knows the difference between men and potato chips (both addictive sub-stances). She knows that "Man," of course, comes from the word "mania," and that, as is the case with too many extraneous potato chips, many men will cause bloating and fullness.

Still, the wise Babe loves love, knows love fluffs up your life expectancy, hitches up your mental knickers, clears the emotional skin, and brings warmth and often jewelry into hours of what would oth-erwise be insipid daytime programming.

And she knows a man may have drawbacks, but his draws can far outweigh them. The possible delightful discovery, on a Machiavellian scheduled "chance drive-by" of his house when he is taking out the garbage, a casual hello, garbage-related chat, coffee, a date, love, lust, skiing in Aspen, and a gift of her own jet on her wedding day are really all today's Babe needs to get by.

Babe Has Tenure in the "University of Love"

The New Middle-Aged Babe has tenure in the University of Love and is wise: she doesn't constantly *label* things going on between herself and a man, use words like "relationship," a bulky, old term refer-ring to intimacies enjoyed by Woody Allen. Nor does she shout around ideas like "totally committed" or "absolutely just friends," as she has learned, things in Middle Age are fluid and weird. Also: *no mere English words describe any state that exists between a man and a woman.*

Though once involved with various men, she sees herself now in nice, simple "emotional trysts," tidy, manageable spates of mutual liking, not requiring endless emotional maintenance, let alone emotional maintenance fees (higher than condo maintenance fees). These "short spates of liking" may get even more delightful and lengthen, but are not required to do so. This is the knowledge midlife brings to Mid-dle-Aged Babes. (*Note:* Mandatory "post-life, side-by-side Graves," bought before a first Valentine's Day, leave this Babe cold.)

How to Tell If You Are Married or Single

No one is happier than the Married Middle-Aged Babe: content, with marvelous children, a wonderful man, an incredible sense of well-being and happiness. Or is she?

Other "Common Symptoms of 'Marriage' in the Middle-Aged Babe"
1. Bored
2. Feel as if you are not with your soul mate

3. Lonely even in a room crowded with family and friends
4. Resentful
5. Believe that you simply "don't connect"
6. Feel disappointed, cheated, confused, let down by life
7. Loneliness, constant thoughts of divorce

Now, let's look at

"Common Symptoms of Being Single in the Middle-Aged Babe"

1. Bored
2. Feel as if you are not with your soul mate
3. Lonely even in a room crowded with family and friends
4. Resentful
5. Believe that you simply "don't connect"
6. Feel disappointed, cheated, confused, let down by life
7. Loneliness, constant thoughts of marriage

One can see, then, how difficult it is to tell which one you are, as the symptoms of both states are practically identical! How to tell the difference? Almost impossible. What does this mean? It means, of course, that being married or single is no indicator of whether you are happy. It also may mean that you are both married and single at the same time.

The Married Middle-Aged Babe

The successfully Married Middle-Aged Babe is wise and giving. She has realized there are things not worth getting upset about, like, for instance, those "breaking news alerts" blazing across a TV screen about a Thunderstorm Alert for the Entire Tri-State Area. She sees difficulty in her marriage *like those,* knowing that, no matter how impressive the prelude, in marriage, as in life, *nothing will ever, ever undo the entire tri-state area or her marriage.* So—come whatever—she blows it off. This "blowing off at will" is a signature trait of the Successfully Married Middle-Aged Babe (and, it might be mentioned, the heroin addict).

Regardless of the low-grade-fever-quality love she may sometimes feel, she does not treat her marriage like a search for a canary, used to detect poison gases in a mine, who is presumed dead.

The Successfully Married Middle-Aged Babe has learned: people, even men, have an inner glow that may not eclipse their lack of an *outer glow*, but, despite difficulties (impending tri-state thunderstorms), can be seen again if one goes in and looks, even digs, with pickax and flashlight through the rubble of previous bad behavior, misrepresentations, interpersonal faux pas, bad counseling sessions, financial misjudgment, romantic misdemeanors, and even romantic felonies.

Sex and the Married Middle-Aged Babe

With sex, the more experienced Married Middle-Aged Babe can be experimental, fabulous, and wild, enjoying many, many, many new forms of sex, available *only* to the experienced Married Middle-Aged Babe, including:

1. **intercourse**—sex with your husband
2. **intracourse**—intercourse, but while on the phone to your friend, even while breathless (claiming, perhaps, to be changing the sheets)
3. **invertacourse**—athletic intercourse, physically arduous, meant to be fabulous and experimental, it is mostly showing off and, despite the noise, no one comes (though couples often "find each other" in the silence after such effort)
4. **introvertcourse**—intercourse after a huge fight, in sullen silence, or while secretly whispering swear words to yourself
5. **incontroverticourse**—total commitment to *this particular act* of intercourse, which absolutely *will be completed* however badly it's going, and in which somebody, even through contentious, torturous effort, will come
6. **invitrocourse**—"intercourse appointments" to have endlessly discussed children, enjoyed by the spouses separately (if enjoyed at all). Invitrocourse's downfall, of course, no expression of love—the physical absence of the spouse, and remarkable intimacy of a strange doctor, plus positional difficulties, make it, though frequent, rarely like "intercourse."
7. **effective decay-preventive dentacourse**—oral sex after using a popular fifties toothpaste

Keeping the "Marriage" in Her Marriage

The Married Middle-Aged Babe's mandate is to retain intimacy, tenderness—to keep the Marriage in her Marriage. So she must do the obvious: keep communications open, perform massage, make mashed potatoes, *and* create an amicable mix of distance and closeness whose yardstick is this: that neither partner ever feels like Moe Howard chasing Shemp Howard around a couch. The sudden appearance of a Moe or Shemp Howard–like figure in a marriage should be taken seriously.

There should be fun in a marriage, an antic quality, but the situation above presents as "requiring counseling." A "Groucho Marx" spouse scooting behind a distraught "Margaret Dumont" contraindicates true intimacy. Other Midlife Marriage Difficulties:

The "Food/Sex Importance Inversion"

In marriage, many Middle-Aged Babe men (and women) experience a "Food/Sex Importance Inversion." Due to age, overwork, or hormonal imbalance, food (or even sleep) may have overtaken sex in a marriage's Desire Quadrant. When the man's deep yearning to make love is matched only by the woman's full-frontal desire for a slice of Death by Chocolate Cake, help is needed.

Taking the Desire Quadrant to a doctor and having it biopsied may provide the only definitive diagnosis. Example: slides from the Desire Quadrant may show (in the woman) large sections of shoes, covered with Linzer tortes and bagels; in men, Burger Kings ringed with scantily clad window-order girls docilely reciting, "That'll be One eighty-nine, pull around." These reveal, conclusively, the presence of The Inversion. Solution?

Desire Quadrant biopsies are a medically ordained "first step," but common sense helps. Sex, like fine bone china, becomes most delicate when "rattled about" in a shaky cabinet (or insecure marriage). The following "Middle-Aged-Babe–Induced" panaceas are suggested:

The Married Middle-Aged Babe must focus on "discovering the new" in sex: Google some retro undies, bring magazine clippings of a "preferable derriere" (e.g., Jennifer Lopez) to a board-certified liposuctionist, and ask him to achieve this with fat from other Babe hind quarters. As well, the Married Middle-Aged Babe knows since deflowering what not to do during sex, but it bears repeating:

What Not to Do During Sex:

Never tell your sex partner he is getting a "Time Out."
Do not shop during sex.
Do not gargle during sex.
Do not sing "Doe, a Deer."
Do not repeatedly guess your partner's weight.
Do not say, "What's that thing?"

Dangerous Categories of Marriage

The Middle-Aged Babe must also learn to recognize several dangerous categories of marriage she won't want hers to slip into, like:

1. The "I Have Topical Ointment on Me, Don't Touch Me" Marriage
2. The "Overscheduled as a Surrogate for Sex" Marriage
3. The "Unmedicated, in Denial, Perimenopausal 'Crash Test Dummy of Her Own Hormones'" Marriage
4. The "In Vitro Madness" Marriage, and
5. The "I'm Faux-Finishing the Outdoor Shower Stall, *That's* What I'm Doing Out Here Till Midnight" Marriage

The Single/Divorced/Widowed Middle-Aged Babe

The Single* Middle-Aged Babe is one of God's very newest creatures. Before, He fully equipped Babes and installed men on all but the raggiest of them. Middle-aged or not, men were as standard as running lights. Now, many middle-aged females are single, whether through choice, defaulting on "Love Loans," or fate. Some are fine with this, choosing fluffy slippers, sweatpants, and a TLC special, "Building an Outdoor Deck Alone," over connubial intrigue. These "Layback Libido Babes" (as they are medically known) can be quite happy, organizing bereavement support groups, holding sales of their old Barbies on eBay for retirement money, having their oil filters checked, and flocking in and out of T. J. Maxx as if they were actually still alive.

For other Single Babes, another standard: Relentlessly Romantic. The true Middle-Aged Babe does not desert her sexual self, leaving it to wander in pathetic wonder, staggering blindly, alone, around that candy department in Blockbuster Video on Saturday night! No, the sexually *soignée* Babe keeps her life with men roiling.

---

* or divorced/widowed

Babe Is *Not* Emma Bovary!

The Middle-Aged Babe may elicit, but does not *need,* her "dream guy," the stuff of high school memories, fantasy lives, the subject of books on Emma Bovary, etc., because the Middle-Aged Babe is a realist, and if she can't be with the one she loves, the canny Babe will perceive what to love in the one she's with (assuming he, prequalified, has already limboed to the level of Minimum Babe Love Requirements).

The new, better, more forgiving, understanding divorced, single, or widowed Middle-Aged Babe enjoys many more people in her life, including herself.

She has, in fact, entirely rethought herself *and* potential men. Her very fabulous "Changing Standards for Men" are so fabulous, they include many marvelous guys she would have never known before, let alone met, let alone given money to on the street they were lying on!

But most critical, and let's be clear here: The Middle-Aged Babe is not some "mercy fuck chick," ragging around life's perimeters like a pathetic, sex-atrophied amateur, digging the local station house talent but unable to score an audition.

In fact, the Middle-Aged Babe *holds* the auditions. She is an active picker, not the passive chosen, shivering with delight when some random guy in aggressively ironed Dockers swaggers over to her at a cocktail party, believing himself "a catch" apparently because he is both *gunning for conversation in fluent English* **and** is *fully dressed.*

No, today's Middle-Aged Babe is not some needy Man-Sucker. She sees men as desirable dessert-like entities she'd love to have, but can frankly take or leave, for, as every American woman alive knows: *there will always be another dessert.*

Indeed, the Middle-Aged Babe has set high, unremittingly stringent STANDARDS for acceptable men, willing to take only the plum few who are "Babeworthy." As we cannot describe the long complex criteria used here, we will instead, for a sense of "feel," show a group of some actual Acceptable and Unacceptable Men for the Middle-Aged Babe.

New Standards

The Middle-Aged Babe takes a new, *Consumer Reports*–like ratings stance on men, as we have here. (*Note:* We road-tested them, threw them against walls (for strength and durability), set them on fire (to see if they were flammable), then whined at them while they were on fire, if that day happened to be our birthday and they had forgotten it (before they were on fire). (See Appendix BB for our newly revised, "Rigorous Testing Standards for The Current Acceptable Babe Man," including features we looked for, male formats we like, and male add-ons we suggest. Being able to add more memory to the male is especially important.)

One important standard in our "acceptability trials": the Middle-Aged Babe has a zero tolerance policy toward one particular "Not-Good-Enough Guy." The criterion: whether he will, one fine day after the relationship is over, cause the Babe to be told by some friend, as the Babe screams her lungs out, "Speed-Moving" his possessions from her place by throwing them out a window, that she is *"just going through the healing process."*

The Middle-Aged Babe *loathes* the healing process, having been through it five, six hundred times depending on the number and volatility of her romances and her age. If she meets you (a guy), sees: nice smile, nice personality, nice politics, *healing process,* you're out of there. The Savvy Babe wants men who *will not cause undue healing* (see upcoming *"Zagat's Guide to All Acceptable and Unacceptable Men for the Middle-Aged Babe Who Walk the Earth"*—with previous spousal/girlfriend ratings, ambience, price, price to the psyche).

Following, to illustrate representative types, is our pictorial essay, "Acceptable and Unacceptable Men for the Middle-Aged Babe":*

---

* Criteria based on actuarial tables, probability charts, digital exams, attendance records, shown in Appendix F. (*Note:* Although specific men may not be currently available, similar ones occur throughout real life.)

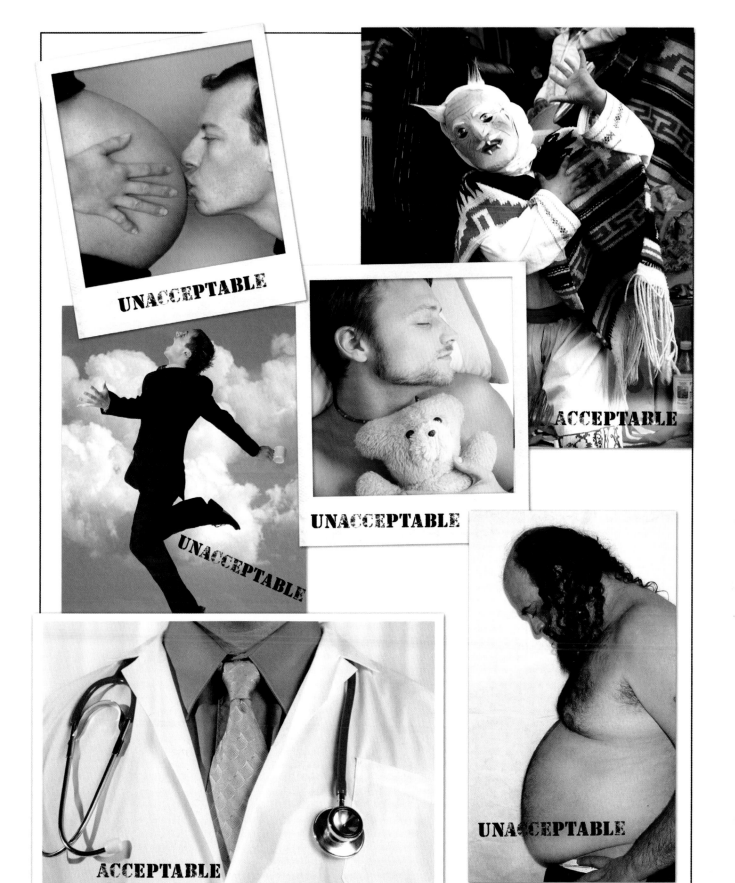

UNACCEPTABLE

ACCEPTABLE

UNACCEPTABLE

UNACCEPTABLE

ACCEPTABLE

UNACCEPTABLE

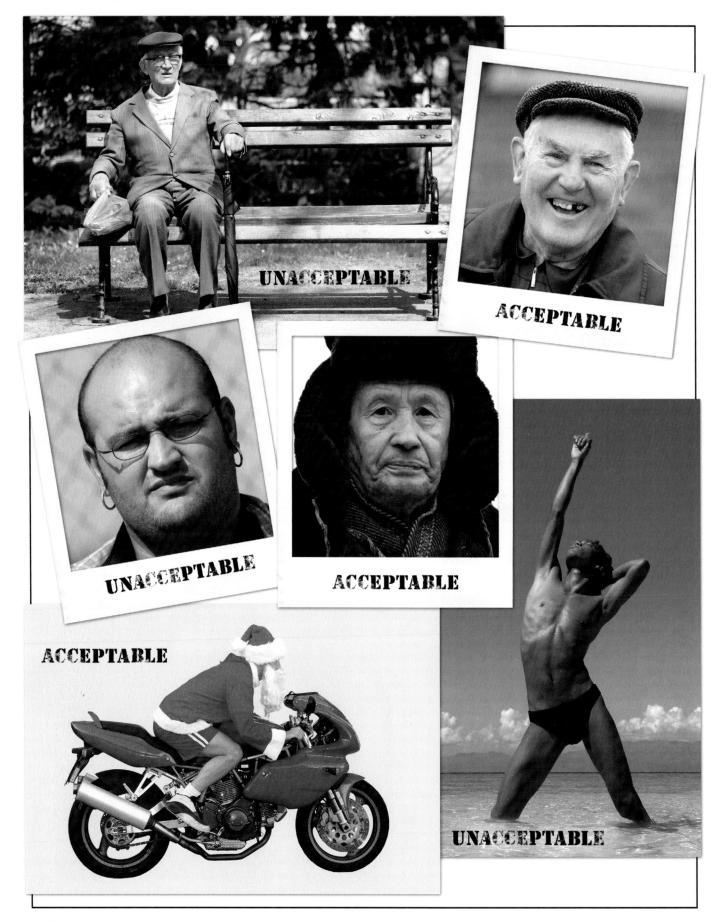

UNACCEPTABLE

ACCEPTABLE

UNACCEPTABLE

ACCEPTABLE

ACCEPTABLE

UNACCEPTABLE

ACCEPTABLE

Laughable: The Idea of "Too Few Single Men"!

Also, the Middle-Aged Babe laughs at the idea that there are too few single men as she has a picture of all of them, which she will share with you here.

These are the remaining single men left on earth, available to the Middle-Aged Babe. Study this, as you will clearly be dating one soon:

Clockwise from left:

James Redmond
Seymoir Bisque
Ignatius Lorrimar
Jack Shein
P. Gustavus Eudora
Bill Hirschberg
Arnold P. Conover
Adam Smigel
Rosario P. De La Soro
Muhammad Ahmet De Suleimann
Schmuel Digany
Jacques de La Fressange
Milos Miscovicz
Constantin Miscovicz-al ha Yamit
Ramon Endotomatassa
Zev Spitzer
Alejandro M. Nativados
Yip Nguyen
Baghdir Muglaiimishaad
MitchWeiner
Yaakov Baskin
Ingmar Sorrensohn
Iliry Haazmat
Lt. Colonel John Boyd Entwistle
Wynton Oscella Ditmars
Wo Dinh Sikh
Hassan Poore
Eugen Flegenheuser
Woto Unger
Bildar Anwat Saleisee
Neil Rosen
Stu Rosen
Dr. Larry Rosen
Ut Basmati Arondahti
Jim Boyd
Sich Omdelkhayyam
John Mulcahy
The Reverend Phil Oster
Jay Katz
Tadische Ortmongenthau
Howard Belkin
Magdar Lopatin
Bill Igles
Benedictus Va Uberthorpenx
Ut Basmati Arondahti
Guy de Baisser
Iso Phat Xzng
Paulo Rodrigues
Josh Myer
Xal Kudo
John Nagelhoffer
Fyodor Putinshka
Ottavio Niarchos
Genghis Sakhjorrgaazahithan
Alberto V. O. Five
Prince Oman Khandahour
Skip Plnes
Janoscz Kapah
William "Bud" McClosky
Iban Bar Ilban
Gil Thomas
John Jacob
Jingleheimer Schmidt
Riaz Malik
Optir Be
Samsat Al Hanan
�᠊ᢇ ᠊ᢇ ᠊ᡶᢇ᠊ᡶᡶ᠊ᢇ
ᢒᢒᡶᢆᡲ ᡶᢆᢎᡶ
§ᢒᢅNH ᢉᡚᢂᢒBBA ᢒᢕᢉᢦᢂᢒᢂAH₁
Gus ✥ᢄ ᢦᢇᢐᢐ ᢇᢅ‛‛ᢅᠴᠵ
Gil Thomas II
Allan Wyckham-Poole
Scheck Bugge
Dan Goldenson
Gilbert P. Williams, D.D.S.
Zolton Rothgar, D.D.S.

The Middle-Aged Babe then knows: there are *not* too few single men. There is an endless supply of men (some of whom may need to be *made* single or otherwise modified).

Thus, the Single Middle-Aged Babe is always either "dating lightly," "dating heavily," or "somewhat married." She is never "sitting out life on the sidelines, pitiful, risk-averse, and solo, like a lone and ugly toadstool in the vast golf course of verdant ups and downs that is Life."

So—excited about new men, but sensitive to her history, the Middle-Aged Babe puts limits on her romantic expectations; she now wears a sort of "psychic girdle." With the acuity of a Maidenform product, this mental Ace bandage "lifts and separates" insane hopes from actual human guy realities. She gives men "second chances" or "do-overs" (as they were called, in technical terms, on the playing fields of youth), meritorious foul shots in real life. Because she knows everyone, of all sexes, is battle-scarred, touchy, hesitant, but mostly, incredibly fucked up.

How to Date

One of the first jobs of the Dating Middle-Aged Babe is to go on dates. While many people have difficulty dating after a long absence from the singles scene, many others have difficulty dating after a *constant presence* on the singles scene. Dating is a social brain teaser, as it requires constantly changing ratios of intimacy and distance, an erotic mental cha-cha choreographed by chemistry, insight, and fear. Uncomfortable? Awkward? Well, let's put it this way—dating is like fucking in a fat suit. Different portions of the brain all look for information (sexual, intuitive, practical), through modes so torturous, a first date can feel like a cross between having a pelvic examination while applying for a small business loan. First dates should require anesthesia, and in some states they do.

Until more desperately needed legislation is passed *mandating* first-date anesthesia, a first date will be an odd couple of hours of wildly scrutinizing and judging the other person, alternately chewing him up deliciously and spitting him out in disgust, while acting completely nice. What a strain! To stick a mental finger down one's throat while laughing gaily!

The "date," especially the initial date, is hard with a large, deep "Expectation Pit" fully surrounding it. To avoid this pit, think of a date as a trip to the library when you were little: you *hoped* you'd find some library books, which you *hoped* you'd *like* enough to go home with. Of course, that wasn't followed by the library books then never calling you, or you Star-Sixty-Nining every hang-up in case it may *be* one of the library books, or later, trying to get *over* the library books, going through the dreaded "grieving process for the library books," and still later, the "healing process from the library books."

Still, if done properly and semi-enjoyed, dates can work. Some rules:

The Middle-Aged Babe's Complete Rules of Dating

Rule #1: You must present yourself quickly—*as you are, but better*—an interesting mix of truth and falsehood.

This mix is best represented by some stores in New York with permanent but emergency-looking signs in their windows that say "Going Out For Business," implying they are "Going Out *of* Business" (a lie), but the signs say "Going Out *For* Business," which we see is certainly true because we notice ourselves go in! A nice, effective mix, then, of truth and falsehood. On a date, you must always be "Going Out For Business."

Rule #2: Blind dates, or fix-ups, are, like, ooooooh, bad, and oooh, they're all, like, scary and weird and awful, wooooh, scaaary. However, as the Middle-Aged Babe knows: *GET OVER IT!*

She knows further: *All first dates are blind dates.* Even if you know the guy and have borne his child, you still don't know him in the date idiom.

Rule #3: The peri-dating period is always more fun than the actual date.

The peri-dating period (like peri-menopause) is the time *before* the actual dating, when there is only meeting and flirting. This is often at some low-pressure social venue, say, the Wawa convenience store self-serve pumps. How sexy! How easy! This is a great time, wherein you seduce, are seduced, joke, dress frantically in expectation of seeing the adored Gas Self-Serving Other: These are the Good Old Days of the date, compared to the date, which will be hell.*

Rule #4: Never ask yourself this question: "Do I ever want him to see my fat?"

Rule #5: Because the only important questions regarding any date are: Is he cute? and Is he insane?

You may wonder: how do I overcome the common "Cute/Insane Conundrum," as it occurs in men throughout the metropolitan and rural world more frequently than any other man-based flaw?

Yes, it's a fact—any man who seems cute, fabulous, and incredible to you *will,* of course, turn out to be insane. It's as certain as "The corn is as high as an elephant's eye," "You can't get a man with a gun," and other Rodgers and Hammerstein–like American realities, such as the one they didn't write a song about: "Oh, What a Beautiful Morning, If *I'm* in Love with Him, He Must Be a Coke Addict!"

The Cute/Insane Axis is a truly scary one, around which many otherwise fabulous men are tightly wrapped. *That his* craziness *is part of his attractiveness* is not lost on the Middle-Aged Babe, who has been there and done that more times than she cares to mention.

(*Note:* That the *first* man after a long, manless period who seems cute and fabulous will *also* turn out to be insane is another Midlife Tenet, as in the Rodgers and Hammerstein song, "The Sky Is Blue, I Love You—Can't We Please *Both* Go to Your Debtors Anonymous Meeting?" or "I Adore a Carousel—Take Off My Underpants Now!" or another favorite, "Oh, I Love the County Fair, and I Understand You're Sober Now, but What Is That Stuff You Keep Sneaking Behind the Ferris Wheel to Drink from My Son's Thermos?") And you can't find out he's crazy in advance *because it's part of the craziness for him to be charming as hell, yet elusive in some incredible hard way you can't figure out.*

You learn only painfully, and much, much too late, that he: still sleeps with his ex-wife, keeps her picture in his car and kisses it at stoplights, invites neighbor ladies for "sleepovers," once slapped his boss, owes his brother 38 million dollars, touches every kitchen appliance forty times before going running, can't eat (food) in front of people, and sticks his finger down his throat after every third meal.

Dating Process in Midlife

Now begins the dating process: a wonderful revelatory time, revealing of just everything, filled with delightful revelations. In fact, by the third date, many men will build into this lovely period, especially

---

* This preferred "Peri-Dating Period" also happens with Blind dates—your friend tells you about the guy, you talk on the phone, draw a breathtaking mental picture—Bliss! You meet and Major El Passo. (Note: To be a thunderous success the date *need only be one-eighth as good* as the peri-dating period.)

for you, almost legally precise elements regarding the revelation of his penis, including the third-date "first look," "right of first refusal," and "most favored nations" clauses, wherein everyone dating him will be given an equal right to see his penis (on the third date), regardless of the level of commitment.

How optimal! This gives the unschooled babe (married many years, only recently divorced) a chance to see a wide potpourri of anatomical styles, including the small handgun-style penis, the Totes umbrella handle–style penis, as well as the umbrella-style, and (as part of this style group) the All-Weather penis (which, frankly, they all are).

First-Date Conversations

To begin dating, one must go through the dreaded "first-date conversation." Understanding what may take place *in advance* goes a long way toward not wanting to leave first dates immediately, mid-conversation. Let's take an example.

Here, a real "first-date conversation" between a Middle-Aged Babe and a fabulous, divorced Israeli man, traveled, prep school in England, Harvard MBA *and* University of Haifa medical degree, now back in Israel, runs family-held oil/natural gas company, netting five hundred million per annum, while alternately (six months each year) volunteering in Doctors Without Borders. Wow! Sterling! Fabulous! Only, five minutes into the evening, stuck in his Mercedes, in traffic, it goes like this:

Him: *(suddenly, loud, like an announcement)* So—what do you theenk of the date so far?
Babe: *(pause)* Well—
Him: *(still loud)* Look—let me tell you what I theenk—I theenk it is going well. How do you theenk it's going? Honestly?
Babe: Fine.
Him: So, good. Look. Let me tell you what I theenk of *you* so far—I find you pheesically attractive. You appeal to the eye. You seem to have many varied interests—I like how you got into the car—what do you theenk of me?
Babe: Well—
Him: Come on! I have told you what I theenk of you, including my perception of how you mounted the car—now you must tell me what you theenk of me—let me tell you what I theenk you theenk—
Babe: Well—you seem—
Him:—I theenk perhaps you like me *before* I ahsk what you theenk of the date so far. I theenk at first you like me, but now you are feeling annoyed with me. I theenk, even a minute ago, you liked me more than you like me right now. Isn't it true that right at thees very second you don't like me? I want you to be honest. Or are you afraid of honesty?
Etc.

At Doctors Without Borders meetings or doing business, this man doesn't act like this. He is, instead, a delightful, caring, border-free doctor with lots to give and much to say. It is just that now, in his "Love Benz," he has lost his mind in the "anxiety envelope" that *is* a first date. Keep this in mind.

Another first-date conversation, with a fabulous foreign filmmaker in New York the Babe met at the 92nd Street Y, where he spoke earlier. The Babe has been invited to his apartment on 125th and Riverside Drive, a crumbling Beaux Arts sublet:

Nestor (the filmmaker): You lahk mah place? Lots antiques. I get, flea markets, auctions, shops. The Vermeer is from Bed, Bath & Beyond.

Babe: Very nice.

Nestor: (drops onto couch) I thought we'd go to the Harley-Davidson Cafe, but I am too weary. (wipes glasses) I saw twelve doctors for it in Paris.

Babe: You lived in Paris?

Nestor: (earnest) Two years ago, I was with Reuters, lived with the filmmaker Françoise Assi, you know her, the cunt? She made that film *The Small Little Wooden Cottage*, a major bitch. You know her? You are her best friend? In any event, due to her, I have a depressed immune system—I won't bore you with details—

Babe: Oh. (quickly) Have you been to the Whitney—

Nestor: (more earnest, yelling, waving arms, intense)—but due to that *super bitch*, who withheld all physical affection even before Sundance—*she* put her film up against *mine*, bringing it with her *other*, *female* lover to the Sundance film festival behind my back!—*She* made my lymphocytes go up not down in response to infection! *She* gave me a lowered immune system, *which* by the way presented as a clinical depression! *And* a constant resistance to pleasure! Anhedonia! The Paris doctor said I had perhaps brought Anhedonia in from Azerbaijan like a parasite in the bowel, but I knew, no, the bitch-cunt caused it! The French doctor cured it with constant, daily gamma globulin shots, every day, for months, while Sundance was choosing between her film and mine, and she, with her other, female lover, out carousing in Aspen as I dealt with excruciating fact of my wife and five children, under arrest in Azerbaijan due to *my* activities, *and* the daily gamma globulin shots, *and* my son being held in solitary, totally apolitical guy, they wanted his laptop which *he* stole from the *bitch's* Paris apartment, believing I had hurt his *mother!* It was hell! Living, fucking hell! Bitch-cunt engendered Hell!

Babe: (deep breath) Do you miss Azerbaijan?

Nestor: Azerbaijan? (tears fill his eyes) Oh, it's beautiful! Like the fine, fierce sex in Paris I once knew, that one time—The Caspian Sea, an unbridled sapphire ribbon threading up into the Caucasus Mountains peaks, which rise, and rise again, from a profuse, wild spurt of edelweiss, to thrust and pierce fiercely, burst, peak after peak, day after day, into the cobalt sky! (leans into Babe's face; tender) Will you go down on me? I would pay you. I mean that only in the nicest way. You seem so right to go down on me. I thought that in the Y, I think it again—Now? I wish it was *before* now, but dahling, I will *settle* for now—

Etc.

Or:

A post-third-date conversation. Fabulous New Guy. You've had first-time sex but, sadly, while New Guy is still living with (though breaking up with) his last girlfriend (so the Babe has become "The Other Woman"):

Babe: *(tearful, into phone)* Is Ron there? *(most wavery possible delivery, near tears)* Hi. Look, Ron, sorry to disturb you at home, and I know you can't talk because your girlfriend is right there so don't worry . . . *(reads from index card)* . . . but not hearing from you for two and a half weeks, due to you needing space to break up with her, out of respect for her, has made me fine but hysterical, because of me needing to hear *your* voice, but you clearly not needing to hear *my* voice, as I'm now clearly calling *you*, and why wouldn't we need to hear each other's voices *equally*, and while I was getting your home phone number online through Google just now, I realized that you don't think of our relationship as anything but a sexual *convenience*, that you have no feelings for me, that all those things you said that night about really wanting to see South Beach and Prague with me were a lie, and I know you can't talk because your girlfriend is in the room, but I am calling to say: I *assume* you actually don't love me, that you are *even* trying to hurt me, and that you will never be with me in Prague or South Beach or anywhere. Is that true?

Ron: No.

Babe: *(still sobbing)* Well, what is true?

Ron: *(long, long pause on the other end of the line; then)* The opposite.

Babe: *(thinks, then, jubilant, starts jumping up and down)* Oh, the opposite! You said the opposite! The opposite! Did you just say the opposite?

Ron: Yes. The opposite.

Babe: Oh, darling! The opposite! The opposite! What a wonderful, beautiful thing to say!

Ron: Yes. Right.

Babe: *(almost singing)* Oh, "The Opposite!" "The Opposite!" Two little words that could make any girl's heart sing like a bird's song in May! The Opposite! I want to shout it from the rooftops, I want the whole world to hear. Oh, "The Opposite!" There is a God!

Relationship Potential

If the Babe, while dating, sees potential for a relationship (that Woody Allen word), it is her job to build it from flirting, through friendship, to closeness, even dearness—you discover you both love clotted cream, French posters, standard transmissions, you're both into conspiracy theories, Edgartown at dusk, the old Fontainebleau Hotel, Tito Puente, Etch A Sketch, Hudson River School landscapes, you're both huge fans of Ronnie Spector, outsider art, new car smell, Gaudí facades, Edward Hopper, Smokey Robinson—and soon, soon you have fallen into a splendid proximity, an intimacy so dear it seems almost remembered, a sweet familiarity that draws you each to the other, in a quiet, deeply felt untrammeled mental place you share with him and him alone in moments of calm and of abandon, so that of course now you must

Give Him a Blow Job

Start too soon and you seem like a slut, start too late or don't start, and you blow the gig; a Blow Job can make or break the neo-affair. It is not that the blow job is requisite; it is just that in sex, it's "what's done," like tipping the waiter, shaking hands over the net, or the after-dinner aperitif (only without the waiter, the tennis court, the aperitif, and your dress).

And the fully realized "Babe As God Intended" is fabulous at all sexual specialties. For what *is* a Babe if not an Austin-Powers-defrosted Bond girl? A semi-geriatric high priestess of orifice-incited ecstasy? Swell blow jobs: centerpiece of the Middle-Aged Babe's sexual œuvre.

But what if it's not? What if the Newly Dating Babe forgot how? Or never really learned—*and, yes, such Babe Anomalies do exist!* The Babe may be reticent, confused about execution, ill-advised as to length of the event or the location and attitude of the teeth or whether or not to talk during it or about it, or unsuccessful in past attempts, choking and begging for air when she should be swooning, moaning, and swallowing with delight. Yes, this—the non-blow-job-fluent Middle-Aged Babe—is the dirty little secret of our ever-changing Blow Job Universe!

Such Babes, naturally occurring, *are* found in nature. (More frequently, perhaps, than the naturally occurring "Blow Job Savvy Babe," also found in nature, fully dressed at birth in micro-mini skirts and thigh-high boots.)

And since the need for a blow job with a fabulous new partner does not creep up on one like a Chanel salesclerk but, rather, arrives like a terrier leaping on a bed, this creates a kind of sexual emergency for the Babe, like a restaurant's sudden need for the Heimlich maneuver, or the necessity to immediately administer CPR at a public pool. Thus, the Middle-Aged Babe could use, say, an emergency poster of that Heimlich type to guide her *at this time.*

It is our contention that an instructive emergency blow job poster be made available to all Middle-Aged Babes against this possibility, so we enclose one here. "The Middle-Aged Babe's Emergency Blow Job Poster" may be hung, like a fire extinguisher, oxygen canister, or other emergency item, on the back of her closet door, a stretch of wall, or any easily accessible place to be used in an oral sex emergency.

It should be positioned so the Middle-Aged Babe may "casually leap" from the bed to read it in an oral sex crisis, then "casually race" back. "Casual hysterical leaping up," of course, must be avoided. One wants a seamless, *offhand* hysterical leap, not to interrupt the flow of the sex.

The Babe perhaps announces a (nonexistent) "phone ringing in the second bedroom," or "faint scent of fire," then races (saunters) to the poster to memorize, memorize, then the offhand slinking back, having not sexually "lost one's place."

(*Style note:* The offhand swagger to casually go read the emergency instructional blow job poster should not be done with the antic mania of that Marx Brother running from Margaret Dumont, but rather with the aplomb of a First Lady welcoming the Harlem Boys Choir to the White House Christmas party.)

And the Babe must remember: Blow Job skills may come, and Blow Job skills may go, but the Middle-Aged Babe's emergency blow job poster always will be there, thinking it knows what it's doing. The Babe may now join *with* the poster, in this attitude, and with numerous film stars who, by the very shape of their lips, indicate their Blow Job Prodigy status, causing our men to privately compare them with us **even though they've never seen them do anything except appear on *Entertainment Tonight* and talk about their life goals!**

And frankly, what better time to finally master the blow job, for the Middle-Aged Babe to flower into the full fold of her oral gifts. For if not now, when, as the pre-heaven period of the sex life is most rewarding; the Posthumous Sexual Athlete, going down on the angels, will most certainly be underappreciated!

The Precariousness of All of Life

Life has shown the Middle-Aged Babe that catastrophe and elation often romp hand in hand.

Thus, the Middle-Aged Babe may find herself head over heels with a man of "advanced age" (and, by advanced, we mean: "*only* 43 when he had the six bypasses," or "*only* 38 when the Toyota flew out of the bushes at him," or "*only* 91 when the ball hit him on the golf course").

These are our ages now: "only 41," "only 52," "only 99," from those stories the Babe hears and occasionally stars in: the young father suddenly felled at the fourth hole, the breast cancer that grew from a pebble to a balloon in an hour, the one-way street/auto-immune disaster, the Barcalounger catastrophe.

Everywhere, everywhere, there is Early Onset Shit—and why shouldn't it invade the Babe sex life? The age of her suitors is higher; the suits of her suitors are bigger; none of this bodes well for "suitor health." And there is no early detection! Of anything! All those 10K walks for diseases, celebrity congressional pleas to fund research, memorial quilts—how can a Babe just go through life in her usual slit skirts, crotchless panties, support hose, and orthotics, when the *un-early-detected catastrophe-to-be* is imminent, and as present in the ecstatic sexual moment as it is in the crypt?

Think for a moment of the Middle-Aged Babe–Man and all the new broken stuff they can find on him now but can't fix, with those celebrated "early detection killjoy" tests like an MRI. New Middle-Aged Babe–Man things like, what, I don't know: "penile arrythmias," "discouraged arteries" (and other conditions, which, if they existed, may lead to heart disease or bladder fibrillation). His "libidinal platelet count" suddenly goes down and God only knows what happens; there could be "sexual strobing," leading to "pinched valves," "overextended testicles," and who knows what-all else!

This greatly concerns the Middle-Aged Babe, who has sewn her share of Memorial Quilts and knows: pleasure and catastrophe are both there, hanging out and just waiting to be introduced!

With this in mind (and with the age of her men on the rise), the vervey, sexy, on-top-of-it, medically happening Middle-Aged Babe requires not only complete information on how to give a Blow Job, but on how to administer CPR and, quite possibly, on how to do both at once. We present here, then, especially for the Middle-Aged Babe who is sexually on the go, "The Middle-Aged Babe's Cardiac Pulmonary Resuscitation During a Blow Job Emergency Wallet Card." Loaded with data on making love and saving lives, the sexually and "catastrophically with it" Middle-Aged Babe gets not only a wall-bound pleasure poster but a guide that travels to wherever things are just about to get fantastic and then go completely to hell (i.e., everywhere).

Like the chart, this card is easily cut out along the dotted lines. It folds into eight parts (with directions and illustrated demonstration) to insert into Babe wallet, for easy access in a roadside oral sex/coronary occlusion emergency. Handy cell phone advised.

Better than any credit card, tell your wallet to cherish what follows.

CPRDBJ (Cardiac Pulmonary Resuscitation During a Blow Job)
Emergency Wallet Card

Step 1: Cut out card along dotted lines. **Step 2:** Follow folding instructions 1 and 2. **Step 3:** Put into wallet.

1. Bi-Fold

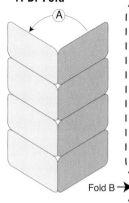

2. Accordion Fold

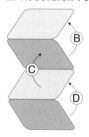

3. Insert into wallet

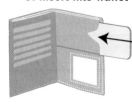

Fold A

Fold B →

Fold C →

Fold D →

1. Remove any obstructions from the throat. (Make sure all airways are clear.)

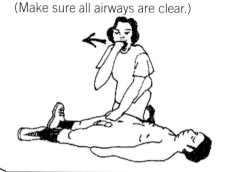

5. Hold penis in both hands. Shout "ARE YOU ALL RIGHT?" Stop. Repeat. Shout. Stop. Repeat.

ARE YOU ALL RIGHT?

2. Place one hand on the forehead and gently push downward so the head tilts backward (to open the airway). Kiss. Repeat. Place penis in mouth. Hold gently for the count of three.

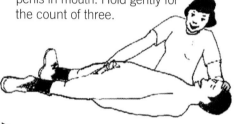

6. Caressing penis, compress chest fifteen times. Bend over and give two breaths, while deep French kissing. Repeat.

15 X

3. Gently circle glans of penis with tongue three times, clockwise. Look, listen, and feel for breathing. If breathing is slow or labored, say, *"Are you all right?"*

ARE YOU ALL RIGHT?

7. Listen for breathing; see if chest and breastbone are rising, falling with faster breathing and penis is increasing in firmness and size. **15 X**

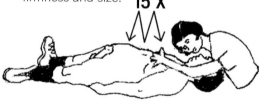

If not, compress chest 15 more times.

4. Place hand on breastbone. If there is no heartbeat, remove penis from the mouth.

8. Thrust mouth over penis, count "1-2-3, 1-2-3," until penis "comes," swallow liquid, appearing to savor it, hike uvula above excess, hold in taste buds.

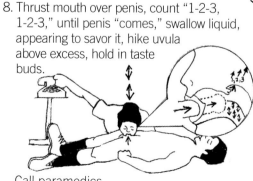

Call paramedics.

GETTING THE LIFE

9. Travel, Entertainment, and New Forms of Fun

Middle Age—wads of bonus "earth time"—allows extended enjoyment of fun things but elongates "doing loathed tasks." First, let's look at some perks—what the "Red Carpet Ready" or "Any Color Carpet Ready" Middle-Aged Babe at her current shocking age can truly, fully enjoy (with the greater wisdom and insights of age, accumulated like free gifts from "Prescriptives") during her new, bonus wads of earth time.

Travel

Travel and Entertainment, escapes to pleasure, nurture the Babe Psyche and are crucial to the Babe Self. "Unworldly" doesn't bespeak a Five-Star Middle-Aged Babe.

But Babe Travel Today lacks the gala, streamer-throwing "Bon Voyage!" aura once de rigueur in a European (or any foreign) spree. Testament to this appears in filmed scholarly research like *Gentlemen Prefer Blondes* and *The Love Boat.* Each portend lush, promising, Andy-Warhol-may-be-on-board levels of fun, back when trunks had stickers and Cameron Diaz wasn't a regular at the Hôtel du Cap. Why?

Our New Wrecked World

It's because our world is now wrecked: shoes must be swabbed and laptops felt up before Babes may board. Fifties-and-before–born Babes know: the world didn't used to be wrecked. At one time, Sandra Dee kissed Pops or Moms and ran with her Samsonite hatbox up the ramp to True Love in France, Italy, Wherever. Now, with Babes having to show picture ID, undo their bras, and point out possible melanomas before boarding, as well as print-their-own-tickets and cook-their-own-Atlantic-spanning-dinners to fly on celebrated El Cheapo modern airlines, some *je ne sais quoi,* elusive glamour has been jettisoned from travel. Travel today has whittled down to this: all Babes simultaneously hurling identical, wheeled, black carry-ons into the sacred Overhead Bin, putting their "seat back" in its sacred Upright and Locked Position, and sitting, upright and locked, for twelve hours. This has ruined the antic, soul-soaring, champagne-soaked trips Travel Fête Babes once knew. Two well-known Middle-Aged Babes—Mrs. Isidor Straus (who went down on the *Titanic*) and Mae West (who probably did the same, only when it was still in drydock)—were never seen putting anything in its upright and locked position, except perhaps their male travel companions in a train sleeper car. Would they stand for today's rigors as springboards to exquisite foreign delicacies, fragrances, edifices, holy places, shopping, and *pay to do it*? I think not.

How to Enjoy Travel Despite Our New Wrecked World

Danger-Junkie Babes grab State Department travel advisories and split to wherever they say "Don't," a highly adrenalized trip, fab scrapbook-to-come (unless you feel your family may flinch, seeing you on the network news, head swathed in gauze holding a sign that says "I am an asshole" in a foreign language, as they enjoy dinner). Still, a Hostage Babe, today's Über Chic Traveler, can dine out on vacation anecdotes for *months,* should she live.

The Road Not Yet Taken and Why

The Middle-Aged Babe visitor in Paris, London, Rome, wants to widen her horizons, but only as wide as the Middle-Aged Bladder will stretch to allow. The Middle-Aged Babe "bladder reach," Babes notice, becomes less and less wide, less elastic. This requires more pit stops on typical days, filled with, say, Shopping and Diet Cokes. On a big Twist 'n' Shout Happening, like a trip abroad, the bladder needs pit stops galore. Indeed, sans infinite "restroom encounters," the bladder becomes surly. And bossy. Given its head, the newly limited Babe Bladder may try to wrest control of Babe destinations, based on ladies' room proximity. The Middle-Aged Babe Bladder may boss around a whole Babe Itinerary. While Odessa, Luxor, and Bangkok seem fab to the Babe, the Babe Bladder (and urethra) may prefer to cut a swath through Wal-Mart, Sears, and Howard Johnson's. The Babe wants to go to Basel and Budapest? The Bladder prefers Prague and the Jo-Ann Fabric Shop. Resolution?

Truth: The Bladder-Driven Travel Plan, if ignored, could force the Middle-Aged Babe to accidentally seek relief on some old temple or sacred burial ground in, say, Thailand. The smug Bladder may laugh aloud as authorities wrest the non–Thai-speaking Babe off to be swathed in gauze on network news for befouling Thai holy grounds. She may be fined, jailed, killed, or denied Sudafed. Such a sojourn, anathema to American Babes, won't do.

In Trip Development, then, the Middle-Aged Babe must *work with* the Bladder.

One way (for the Dexterous Babe) is to use a compass, lie on the floor on a map of her desired destination, place the compass needle on her Bladder, then draw a circle on the map between her Bladder and her Destinations (for example, the distance from the Bladder to Copenhagen or the Bladder to Buenos Aires, etc.). Then Babes must unearth ladies' rooms (in new and old Michelin or Frommer's guides) that fall within circled areas. This lying-on-maps, outlining-local-ladies'-rooms-with- your-bladder-as-ground-zero, sadly, must be central to Foreign Jaunts. True, you may have to lie on thirty maps. But the Wise Babe, having contained a bladder inside her previously, knows—out of town, *she must know where her next ladies' room is coming from.* (*Note:* Given that foreign countries serve stiff espresso, a powerful diuretic, the Bladder Itself may clamor to voice *its own* Preferred Treks.) An arc in ink should then be drawn from the Babe Bladder to the first known rest stop in the *Bladder's* "pick city," highlighted in yellow, and highlighter lengths compared between locales the Babe craves and those the Bladder champions. Yes, this is difficult. Thus, we present here, for the first time, the much needed, "The Middle-Aged Babe's Worldwide Map of Ladies' Rooms." This map shows Ladies' Rooms' exact locations globally. Culled from travel guides, newsreel footage, workers in the field, microfiche from high-flying State Department espionage planes, and with the help of Chambers of Commerce from Rabat to Istanbul, this map includes even elusive "comfort stops" behind souks, into the Bay of Bengal, near pay phones, in tall pampas grass, and even on hard-to-flush tundra.

The Middle-Aged Babe's Worldwide Map of Ladies' Rooms

= All known Ladies' Rooms by continent.

For the Domestic Traveling Babe:
Direct Air Routes to Acceptable Ladies' Rooms in the U.S.

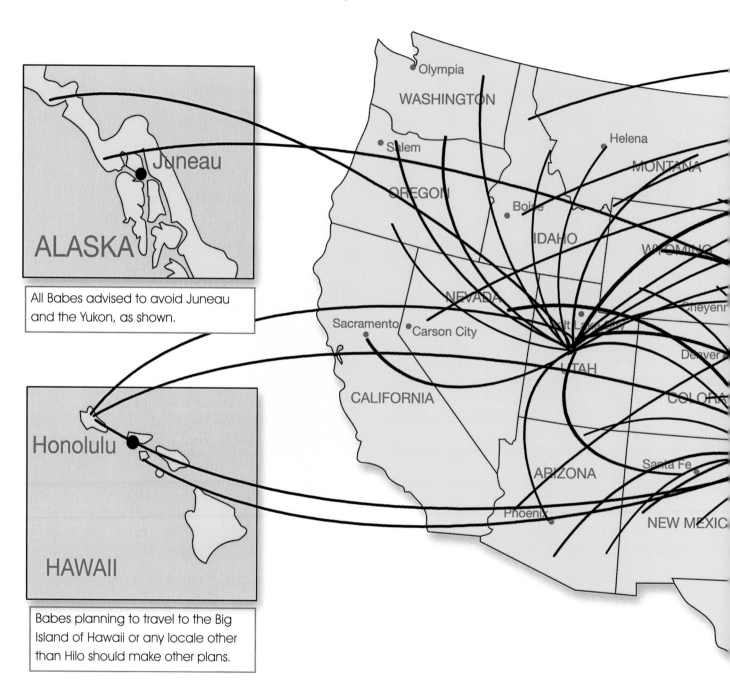

All Babes advised to avoid Juneau and the Yukon, as shown.

Babes planning to travel to the Big Island of Hawaii or any locale other than Hilo should make other plans.

Family reunions, emergencies, and graduations may mandate other destinations than, say, Providence (rife with Babe-friendly restrooms), Pierre, South Dakota, or Oklahoma City. Even if the wedding is *not* in Pierre, South Dakota, hygiene-hip Babes may stop there, then hire a private plane to her true destination (Los Angeles). An admittedly pricey, but truly germ-free route. Priceless!

Yes, even in restroom-rich America—stop at a *good* Ladies' Room in Austin, Texas; then take a "puddle jumper" to your son's graduation in Des Moines. Easy, avoids ignitable "hot-air hand dryers," and the Des Moines flight *may* have a movie!

Other Babe World Travel Needs

Many Middle-Aged Babes want "acceptable" (i.e., Classic American* "Employees Must Wash Hands" Type Public Facilities). Such places, even stateside, occur only in Upscale Department Stores or attendant-hand-towel-doling-out evening spots (some countries don't even *have* evenings, just curfews). Bolder Babes make do with "devil-may-care hygiene"; others avoid, well, the world.

Third-World Chic

Bolder Babes can swing with "Less Bad than Bathing with Rattlesnakes" foreign hygiene. Propaganda leaflets doubling as toilet paper, "toilets" without seats, easily plunged into, and hilarious refrigeration laws, so that huge sides of beef hang in 90-degree marketplaces for days, must be seen as "fabulous ethnic touches." Babes must act cool, as if they were always around sides of beef hung in 90-degree heat and this is just another of those dull times. Instantly Indigenous Babes get their heads around the Flies Everywhere look: it's only polite to the beef, its vendor, and the momentary government.

Restroom Hazards for Babes

Microscheduling trips in order to touch down *only* at "OK restrooms" is not easy, even in restroom-rich America. And the Perimenopausal Babe (trusting "iffy ovaries") who conceives requires "Changing Tables." Weight-conscious Babes freak at "reflected love handles"in Fat Mirror Facilities here and abroad. Our map of "Direct Air Routes to Acceptable Ladies' Rooms in the U.S." with appropriate amenities (thanks to polling, volunteer spot checks, and, again, microfiche from high-altitude State Department spy jets) enhances Babe Mobility.

In the U.S., of course, restrooms can be found in stores, restaurants, and public parks. In New York, surprised visitors may find it necessary to convert "covert" locales into restrooms, as the city is public-facility shy. Traffic, in a rented car, may encourage the saving of large soda cups for desperate, disposable use during hour-long waits outside tunnels. Traffic, of course, is part of the fun 'n' toxic ambience of New York, and joining in native New Yorkers' solutions embraces the "zen" of its regional magic.

---

* The "Classic American" ladies' room brings to mind Babe Friend Gilda Radner, who in the sixties traveled with her guy and a "hippie couple," sleeping outdoors across the U.S. The only American Restrooms were in Amoco stations, and Gilda, envying the "wild ways" of the hippie chick, who'd never paper the seat or do any bourgeois thing, inspired Gilda to swing and follow suit. Thus, from New York to Ohio, through Kansas, the Dakotas, and Montana, into and out of Vancouver, down the Pacific Coast Highway and into L.A., Gilda didn't paper the seat. On the last stop in L.A., she happened to share the ladies' room with the hippie chick, who took one look at her nonpapered seat and yelled, "*Eeeewwwwww,* that's disgusting! I'd never sit on one of those without papering the seat! Can you *imagine* what you would catch?" Gilda, though humiliated for years, caught nothing, thank God.

How to Lie on a Beach Fully Dressed

The Taj Mahal, Macy's, Azerbaijan—tempting locales, but which for which Babes? "Go Babes" like to shop, see, eat. The above destinations are perfect, except Azerbaijan, which, while "go," may also require some running.

Your Costa Ricas, your St. Barts, your South Beaches are for Babes who, remarkably, *are able to not think, read, or talk but can engage in a rare activity called "relaxing," or "lying on the beach."* This doesn't automatically arm Babes with "Display Bods" they can happily array on the sand for appreciative passersby. Such Babes, then, *must lie on the beach fully dressed.* Or throw that (essential!) choir robe on the ground, and wriggle in. Alternately, lie down in black pants, Ralph Lauren cashmere turtleneck, cummerbund, boots, and catch some rays!

Babe Travel Drug of Choice

Disneyworlds of adulthood, outlet malls are loved by Babes who'll make U-turns on turnpikes to avoid missing one and are optimum travel destinations. But, while Premium Outlet Malls and High-End Couture Clearance Centers dot this great land of ours, indeed make it great, only New York's Woodbury Commons has Chanel. Forget Prada, Fendi, and Missoni (unless Babes tour outlet malls in Switzerland—a real Babe treat: see Appendix I for info).

Given this, we've found, near a Days Inn and Key Largo "grassy airstrip," the Middle-Aged Babe's Ultimate Destination: in "Outer Basin, Florida," open only in hurricane season, surrounded by a moat of starving alligators, it's the Middle-Aged Babes' "Outer Basin *Really* Premium Outlet Mall." The drawbridge opens once, at 4:00 a.m., for two minutes, permitting selected entrants yanked in by former velvet-rope employees from Studio 54 to enter, but *is so worth the two- or three-day wait on that drawbridge.* (*Note:* Men are allowed only if they stay in the Food Court or at the Taillevent Outlet or the Le Cirque Outlet, the Harry Cipriani Outlet, or the P. Lorillard Outlet.)

Other than the Hermès Outlet, the Louis Vuitton Outlet, the Sub-Zero Outlet, the Bone Marrow Outlet, the Plasma Outlet, the Ferrari/Bugatti Outlet, the Next Season Versace Outlet, and the Next Season After *That* Donna Karan Outlet, our favorites include:

- **The "U.S. Mint Outlet."** They carry fabulous dollar bills from a few seasons back, but you absolutely can't tell: here, five (last season's) dollars cost two dollars, and if they're having a sale, you can get six (two seasons ago) dollars for a dollar and a half! Or ten (multi-seasons old) dollars for three dollars (which look absolutely au courant). Most people really try to load up here, making numerous trips to the car. There is even a Bargain Bin, with, for example, "three ten-dollar bills for a dollar" (many seasons old), but it can contain some real finds, like classic hundred-dollar bills, thrown in by inattentive sorters.

- **The "Change Your Ticket Anytime, Do Whatever You Want, Super Saver Airline Ticket Outlet."** This outlet specializes in Super Saver fares on all major airlines, but leftover, old ones, unfilled seats from, say, 1994, are here for a tenth of their original Super Saver price. True, you can't use them, as the flights landed years ago, but the prices are marvelous and you can change the departure dates as many times as you want at no extra charge! Talk about Super!

- **"The Old, Used Dog Outlet."** Last season's pups, rejected by visitors to the pound, may find homes here. While the dog's shape may be slightly "outré," the tail angles vintage sixties or seventies, the noses are just as wet as this season's dogs', and many are paper trained. Even "seasons ago" dogs can be made to look up-to-date great with the addition of a "this year's look" collar (from the Burberry Dog Collar Outlet).

- **The "New Birth Order Outlet."** Grab your siblings' birth certificates and get mucho dollars off this product from seasons and seasons ago—the order of your births! Birth order, of course, preordains how much success you will have in life and can be reordered here, then printed on a "government document," T-shirt, or colorful tote, to drive the point home to your siblings again and again. Perfect gifts!

- **"1950s American Air Outlet."** Vintage Air is really so much better than our air now. Filled with real oxygen and, interestingly, said to have been filtered through a one-time "ozone layer" that the earth supposedly "once had," there are no visible particles floating in this air anywhere! How vintage! This fabulous, see-through antique air can be breathed by anyone, even emphysema patients, and its lovely clear color matches anything. Grab a canister or mask, give as gifts.

- **The "American Express Travelers Cheques Outlet."** Last year's travelers checks: previously ten dollars for a ten-dollar check, here they're nine dollars. Hundred-dollar checks are ninety dollars, and five-hundred-dollar checks are, for some reason, free! A wonderful choice.

- **The "Cyclamates Outlet."** This low-cal sweetener, illegal in the United States but still available in Canada, can be gotten here (who knows how?). At a dollar a pallet, the Babe can stock up on artificial sweetener that tastes exactly like sugar, and though she will have hundreds and hundreds of pallets she can move furniture on the side. Everyone knows that's how they all have fabulous thighs in Canada, so what's the FDA's problem, right?

- **The "Escada Outlet Outlet, the Chanel Outlet Outlet, and the Prada Outlet Outlet."** Items from seasons and seasons ago, which have gone unsold in Escada, Chanel, and Prada outlets elsewhere may be found here at a fraction of their original price and a fraction of their original color and style. In fact, a fraction of their original fabric may be left, requiring a jeweler's loupe and/or large magnifying glass to recognize what item you've found. Sometimes, *they may pay you to take it* (whatever "it" is).

- **The "Totes 'Rain Hair' Outlet."** Totes (of the see-through rainboot one wears, causing it to appear as if you're really wearing just shoes), produced a line of "Rain Hair" to be worn over your own hair, as if you weren't wearing anything at all, but stay styled perfectly in a driving downpour! Still, though frizzproof, water-resistant, unmoving even in a 100-mile-an-hour wind, it failed to sell, as it came only in red, a color natural to few but Mrs. Totes, its inventor. Still, incredibly well priced. Can be combed (once, maybe).

Visitors' Guide to The Outer Basin Premium Outlet Mall*

*All cars not removed from public parking sub-dungeon by 9:41 p.m. will be kept.

The Outer Basin Premium Outlet Mall*

Outer Basin, Florida

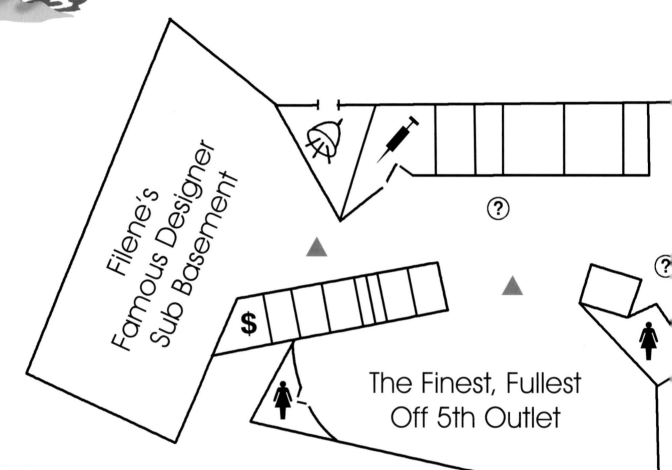

Filene's Famous Designer Sub Basement

$

?

?

The Finest, Fullest Off 5th Outlet

- The Hermès Outlet
- The Louis Vuitton Outlet
- The Sub-Zero Outlet
- The Bone Marrow Outlet
- The Adoptable White Baby Boy Outlet
- The Plasma Outlet
- The Ferarri/Bugatti Outlet
- The Next Season Versace Outlet
- The Next Season After *That* Donna Karan Outlet
- The U.S. Mint Outlet
- The Change Your Ticket Anytime, Do Whatever You Want, Super Saver Airline Ticket Outlet

- The Old, Used Dog Outlet
- The New Birth Order Outlet
- The 1950s American Air Outlet
- The American Express Travelers Cheques Outlet
- The Delta, US Airways, Continental Expired Points Outlet
- The Cyclamates Outlet
- The Escada, Chanel, Prada Outlet Outlet
- The Totes "Rain Hair" Outlet
- The Yves St. Laurent Outlet
- The Gucci Outlet
- The Tom Ford Outlet
- The Taillevent Outlet

* Note: Men are permitted in "The Outer Basin Premium Outlet Mall" only if they stay in the Food Court at the Taillevent Outlet, or the Le Cirque, or Harry Cipriani Outlet. In this area, also, seating arrangements of wonderful comfy couches, and TV sets, and an enormous number of remotes, far more than the number of TV sets, so the viewer may pass quite a pleasant hour trying to guess which one works on which set, or works at all! This marvelous divertissement, coupled with a special, anniversary edition of the fifties magazine, *Making Good Time* (for drivers), and a goodly amount of Perrier Jouet (for those who can find it, rolling, as it so often does, under the couches, with the help of our staff!), can occupy the Male visitor to the Mall for hour upon delightful hour!

Mall Services

- **?** Information Booth
- ▲ "You Are Here" Guide
- Restrooms/Birthing Chambers
- Detox Centers
- **$** Currency Exchange (Cambio)
- Emergency Cuticle Repair
- Rickshaw Driver Deployment Center
- Chauffeur Showering Area

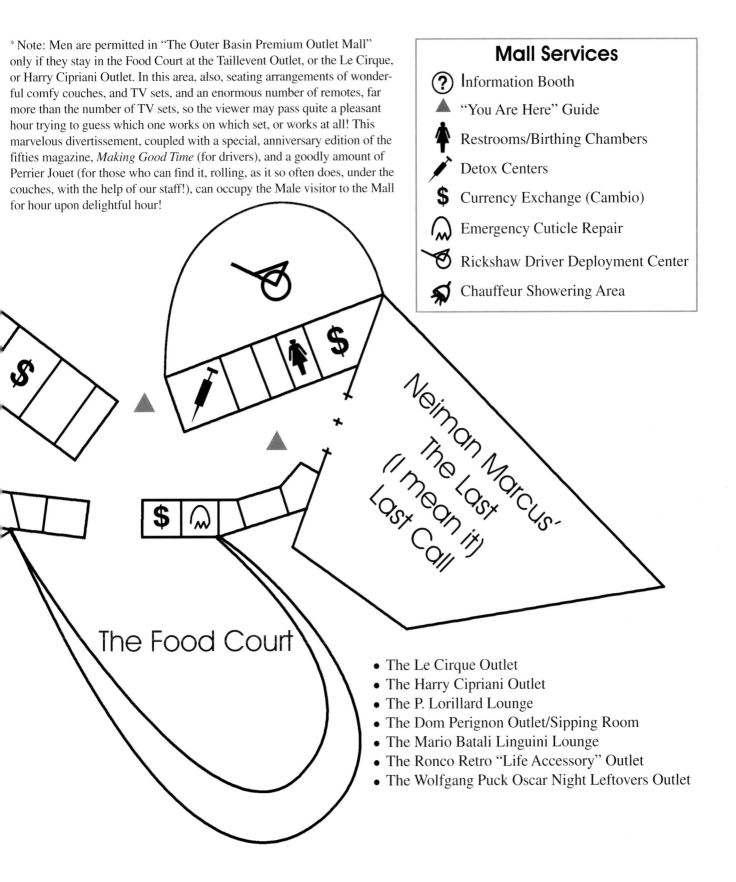

Neiman Marcus'
The Last
(I mean it)
Last Call

The Food Court

- The Le Cirque Outlet
- The Harry Cipriani Outlet
- The P. Lorillard Lounge
- The Dom Perignon Outlet/Sipping Room
- The Mario Batali Linguini Lounge
- The Ronco Retro "Life Accessory" Outlet
- The Wolfgang Puck Oscar Night Leftovers Outlet

Entertainment

Entertainment, once available in bulk, by, say, putting your underpants on your head and moaning like a ghost, or pulling people's fingers and making fart sounds, appears to have left the American scene. Once we soared with it—Sunday Night was *Ed Sullivan*, Saturday was *Mary Tyler Moore*—days didn't have names then, just shows, to identify them. Every day was *Captain Kangaroo, Bandstand, Johnny Carson.* Entertainment smashed open our console-style TV set doors, burst from our local theaters—*Exodus* (one actually entered this, didn't leave as title suggests), *West Side Story, On the Waterfront, Meet Me in St. Louis*—(*note:* best movies had geographic directions in their titles)—shook the very souls of our theaters (when theaters had souls) and ourselves, wrenching actual human emotions from fictions—real tears, real laughter, real gasps, real applause. Oh, that was Entertainment, and boy did we have it! Soul-shattering, rafter-shaking, pulse-liquidating Entertainment that could change a Plain Kid to a Kid With a Dream (the Dream of Being a Star!).

Here's what we have now—nothing. Movies starring people with neither faces nor names enabling you to tell them apart, and many, many TV shows about decorating other people's houses, swapping houses and decorating them, decorating houses without telling the people, decorating houses and then selling them, and decorating houses, then selling them without telling the people. Should movies morph into this form on TV, shows may one day feature Dustin Hoffman, Dame Judith Densch, Barbra Streisand, and Anthony Hopkins learning how to stencil-paint walls in a flower motif, make a new sofa out of a lamp, a lamp out of a sofa, then surprising Sydney Pollack with the fabulous results, having sold his house first, surprising him even more. This will be Entertainment.

The Midde-Aged Babe, then, is stuck in the Entertainment-free Purgatory Today's Show Business has become, entertainment like some sleep-inducing cat's cradle of either watching walls get painted a rich, vibrant peach or turning the channel and watching a NASCAR (or foreign person) burst into flame. *Saturday Night Live* and *The Simpsons* reruns supply some relief; but other entertainment options don't appeal to the one-time Screen Loving Babe, who avoids TV sets and Cineplexes like bad restrooms.

Concerts

Rock star divas go in and out of rehab like Babes go in and out of their garage, often shave their heads (females), but, worse, CAN'T SING OR DO ANYTHING MILDLY ENTERTAINING. Many are also so thin as to be mistaken for onstage electrical cables, so sometimes perform unseen. This is anathema to Babes, who aren't entertained by the cost of the tickets, don't know the words to the songs, or even which ones *are* the songs. Going to hear older stars audibly pick up a couple mil for an hour's work (they put the sound of paying the star in cash, and of the star counting it aloud, through the amps as a quick sound check before show time, if you listen closely). Still, slightly better. But old stars lip-syncing "old favorites" brings tears to eyes of many Babes, as such songs remind her of lost loves, lost luggage, or vaginal infections and their once-loved sources. "Farewell Tours" by groups or individuals, who will be making "*Final* Farewell Tours" immediately after, also a ripoff. But such celebrities often have "musical talent," can "sing," "play instruments," or "change costumes constantly for no reason" in a riveting, professional way. Some have lighting designers, and people who design them, themselves. Crisscrossing colored lights, passing constantly through the venue as if leading a 747 to land there, lost their "hypnotic thrall" for Middle-Aged Babes in 1974. Lighting designers for real legends, after much thought, *can think of other things to do with the lights.*

Movies

"Independent films," "Merchant Ivory Productions," and anything with "Garfield" comprise top-tier, Cannes-worthy Babe entertainment. Other films, with sex, violence, and dance (often indiscernible from one another), Babes hate. Movies full of "acting" are particular horrors, as national publications disclose the actors' true, deeply icky selves, descriptions Babes can't shake. Young actors—all identical, with identical names, faces—may be obfuscated in films by gifted directors (James L. Brooks, Steven Spielberg, Scorsese, Pollack). *Their* challenge—telling the "actors" apart to call them to the set *by name.*

New York City

New York City now has been made a theme park of its former self—same landmarks, taxis—but they redid Times Square to be "cute" and "well lit" instead of appropriately seedy, scummy, and prostitute-ridden (major drag; avoid!). Entertainment tip—NYC school plays! Often the same as Broadway revivals (like *Our Town, Jesus Christ Superstar, 42nd Street, All My Sons*) but they have big stars of the future in them and at one-hundreth the price.

Babes may applaud in their homes, privately, after reruns (*SNL, The Simpsons*) but may have to wait till two, three in the morning to see them. (Use DVR: set time, push "record" button—applaud alone midday!)

Fun

What is Fun?

Fun takes the Babe out of her head and puts her, without moving, in more pleasant surroundings. It's a vacation from the mind. Unlike Travel, "Fun" may be had sitting still, in an hour, a night, or an afternoon.

Many Babes fear at this age they may be "running out of new fun," or they may have used up their allotted supply. Still, they need not yet move on to what they fear: Full-time, Heavy Lifting, Painful, Go-for-it Aging.

In fact, Middle Age (Bonus Fun Time) *mandates* new Babe Fun. Tap-dancing class, yoga, trashing your ex-husband (while others listen and nod), photography, picnics, découpage, serial marriage, Late Life Smoking, extreme boxing, extreme skydiving, extreme bowling, and more top the "Babe New Fun" list!

Other New Middle-Age Fun

Having gorged on fun previously (the sixties), Middle-Aged Babes must revel in contemporary fun, hip now. Computers—dating, shopping, e-mailing, crashes—discussed loudly on buses, planes, or the Metroliner with hip-tech brawny young guys using *soignée* terms like *USB port* and *Mouse* is great, au courant fun.

Other Middle-Aged Babe Fun: "Staying Awake," "Swinging Hard Before 9 p.m.," "Learning How to Sit on Cement Steps at Concerts," "Continuing to Get Paid Past Forty."

Cruises (to see whales in Alaska; Tahiti to buy black pearls; Singapore to uncover terrorist cells) are fun but riddled with "Cruise Food!" These Buffets *can be no-weight-gain fun,* if the Babe (as Socialites, pre–dinner parties, have always done) uses one trick: *eat before leaving on the cruise!!* Other Cruise Fun? "Testing for Rising Temperatures of the World's Oceans to Prove Global Warming" (*note:* requires a meat thermometer tied to a jump rope and some drunk guy who'll hold your ankles). Also fun: "Trying Not to Fall in While Some Drunk Guy Holds Your Ankles." Tennis, bridge played for money (à la Barbara Stanwyck in *The Lady Eve,* a Classy Cruise–Period film, a good style guide for how to act, dress, and *be* on cruises). Other Cruise-Film Chic to emulate: *The Palm Beach Story* (director Preston Sturges), *An Affair to Remember* (director Leo McCarey), *Gentlemen Prefer Blondes* (director Howard Hawks), and Fred Astaire's *Royal Wedding* and *Shall We Dance?* are perfect style guides to natty cruise dress, behavior, dance styles, circa 1930–1950. Get noticed—you'll be the only one tap dancing in black and white.

Getting rich in a big hurry, also "Babe Fun," can be achieved legally. (See "Middle-Aged Babe Relationships" chapter, the section on "How to Erase a Prenup from His Lawyer's Hard Drive." Also, under "Finances," check out "Lotto" in the pie chart.)

More Fun: Books

In Middle Age, some summer, the Babe may finally (!) catch up on a brief list of books she has always meant to read, skipped, almost read only never did, was supposed to in school but "shit happens," etc. Having CliffsNotes'd them to pass the finals, or blown them off, opting for "incompletes," such Incomplete Babes may now realize a "literary level playing field" with peers. Our list (based on polls, demographic research, tapped Babe phones, and grade points from the "Middle-Aged Babe College Graduation Period") are a slight, whimsical diversion, taking up only about one half of her life. (Could supplant boring sleep.) Fun? You betcha!

Babe Fun Reading List

Sons and Lovers
The Sound and the Fury
As I Lay Dying
The Purloined Letter
Being and Nothingness
L'Étranger
Oedipus
Madame Bovary
The House of the Dead
Remembrance of Things Past
The Castle
The Bobbsey Twins at the Seashore
Idiot's Delight
Critique of Pure Reason
Tess of the D'Urbervilles
The Sun Also Rises
The Bobbsey Twins Take Up Canoeing
Death in Venice
Thanatopsis
The Tales of Scheherazade
Twenty Thousand Leagues Under the Sea
The Age of Innocence
Notes from the Underground
The Golden Bowl
The Count of Monte Cristo
A Portrait of the Artist As a Young Man
All of Chaucer
The Man in the Iron Mask
Wuthering Heights
Dr. Faustus
Silas Marner
The Mill on the Floss
The House of Mirth
The Odyssey
The Oxford English Dictionary (all volumes)
The Brothers Karamazov
Spanish for Beginners
Rabbit, Run
Sentimental Education
Absalom, Absalom!
The Talmud
The Picture of Dorian Gray
Moby Dick
Seize the Day
Tartuffe
The Hunchback of Notre Dame
Daisy Miller
Aesop's Fables
The Aeneid
Anna Karenina
The Loved One
One Hundred Years of Solitude
The Red and the Black
Ulysses
The Magic Mountain
The Portrait of a Lady
Metamorphosis
Under Milk Wood
Light in August
Cherry Ames, Student Nurse
War and Peace
Donna Parker, Star-Spangled Summer
All Quiet on the Western Front

A Farewell to Arms
A Distant Mirror: The Calamitous Fourteenth
    Century
Autobiography of Malcolm X
Bury My Heart at Wounded Knee
Born on the Fourth of July
Cry, the Beloved Country
Crime and Punishment
The Chosen
The Autobiography of Benjamin Franklin
The Ascent of Man
The Adventures of Huckleberry Finn
The Complete Poems of Emily Dickinson
Don Quixote
The Death of Artemio Cruz
Doctor Zhivago
Democracy in America
Death of a Salesman (in English and Chinese)
Eyes on the Prize: America's Civil Rights
    Years, 1954-65
Farenheit 451
Frankenstein
Favorite Folktales From Around the World
Go Tell It on the Mountain
Gulliver's Travels
The Great Gatsby
The Grapes of Wrath
Great Expectations
Hamlet
Heart of Darkness
Hiroshima
Invisible Man
Ivanhoe
Invisible Men: Life in Baseball's Negro
    Leagues
Jane Eyre
The Jungle Book
Long Day's Journey Into Night
Look Homeward, Angel
Lord of the Flies
Main Street
The Member of the Wedding
Mother Courage and Her Children
Macbeth
My Antonia
No Exit
Native Son
Profiles in Courage
Pride and Prejudice
Père Goriot
A Passage to India
The Red Badge of Courage
Robinson Crusoe
The Silent Spring
The Scarlet Letter
The Time Machine
The Tin Drum
The Trial
Uncle Tom's Cabin
Waiting for Godot
Walden
Winesburg, Ohio
Beowulf

The Adventures of Augie March
Death Comes for the Archbishop
The Last of the Mohicans
A Tale of Two Cities
Armies and Societies in Europe, 1494-1789
The Art of War
An American Tragedy
Tom Jones
The Good Soldier
The Turn of the Screw
To Kill a Mockingbird
Babbitt
Bartleby the Scrivener
Swann's Way
The Crying of Lot 49
Cyrano de Bergerac
Call It Sleep
Vanity Fair
Gravity's Rainbow
A Rage to Live
The Fall of the House of Usher
Green Eggs and Ham
The Plague
Cinderella
Naked Lunch
The Golem
Pal Joey
The Taxi That Hurried
Butterfield 8
Nancy Drew and the Mystery of the Old Well
Réflexions sur quelque points de littérature
Pat the Bunny
Tropic of Cancer
The Little Foxes
Another Part of the Forest
Marjorie Morningstar
Eloise
Billy Budd
El Hadj
The Tell-Tale Heart
Thus Spoke Zarathustra
Nancy Drew and the Mystery of How to Get
    Out of her Blue Roadster
On the Road
The Caine Mutiny
The Hat on the Bed
Mazel and Schlimazel
A Tree Grows in Brooklyn
The Second Sex
Nancy Drew Gets Her First Strapless Dress
    Ever, the Mystery of How
The Instrument
Washington Square
The Cat in the Hat
Watch on the Rhine
Appointment in Samarra
Pierre and Jean
Little Women
Little House on the Prairie
Little Engine That Could, The
The Only Possible Argument in Support of a
    Demonstration of the Existence of God*

* **Babes who *did* the reading in school and thus had far, far richer adult lives with a greater capacity for love, purpose, resonant insights, and a far deeper appreciation of beauty in life, Our World, and those around her may skip above "Fun."**

10. Middle-Aged Babe Relationships
Old and New Friends, Boyfriends, Family, Extended Family, Overextended Family

A cacophony of relationships surround today's Middle-Aged Babe. Friends, family, former family, former-family-to-be, and, not surprisingly, random "unfinished-relationship personnel"— forgotten children from a previous marriage, ex-spouses making endless, unreturned calls to you, "swinging" realtors you meet downsizing your digs post-divorce, Fix Ups who got all the furniture in their divorce but are herpes carriers, girlfriends who owe Babes three dollars from 1969, now on Step Five ("get forgiven by everyone") in their twelve-step program and call many times daily—this "friendship detritus" rattles around the bottom of a Babe's life, "emotional loose change," "psychological purse fuzz." Needy intruders, hot for Babe reconnection, may try to glom on to Babes as old, but now new, "Babe friends." "Relationship debris" thereby clogs Babe "Friend Arteries," through which dangerous "friendship clogs," unchecked, can go directly to the heart.

Losing bad "Past Friends" can save Babe Lives, make room for upcoming friendships and male liaisons in the Babe's ever-changing job/living/geographic/ marital status.

Friends Old and New

Good "Vintage Friendships" are supports, requisite to Babes feeling "known," "understood," or even "just tolerated." Upkeep is cheap: e-mail, free long distance on some cell phones—but these friendships *require* Babe maintenance. To know one "has been tolerated before" will make one believe one can "possibly be tolerated again," or even "loved." Also, old plastic surgery secrets and behavioral misdemeanors find safe haven with trusted old friends (unless the Babe is a movie star and the friend sells her story to the *National Enquirer*).

Choosing New Friends

Qualities to Beware of

1. Regional accent

2. Size of hair (too big or small)

3. Choice of "Status" or "Normal" purse

4. Constant wearing of flip-flops or stilettos

5. Endless reports on compliments paid to pending friend's "fabulous-for-her-age-heart" by her doctor (or worse, a "specialist"), and "frequency of generalized bragging" suggests a pending friend Babe should lose now.

6. Re: men: does the new friend "recycle" them?

7. Count times potential friend says: "Vicodin," "stash," "Lithium," or "heroin," as related to her daily lifestyle.

8. Also, balance this pre-friend's compatible appetite, sense of humor, and number of relatives in the jewelry and oncological professions, pre-friendship.

New "Friends" to Avoid

1. Fifty-year-olds with one-year-old kids
2. People whose sex you can't discern
3. People who, on leaving banks, jump in your car with a black sack screaming, "Gun it!"
4. Those who disclose their insatiable appetite for sex in Dumpsters

What to Do with Old Friends

In the case of old friends, reconnection often kicks in immediately after initial encounter. Find commonalities you both once enjoyed, like:

1. Trashing anyone who's thin
2. Watching the Weather Channel together with worried expressions, while each calls relatives in high-risk areas on cell phones, endlessly
3. Organizing the inside of every closet in every residence of either friend (exception: closets in the rooms of "resident minors")

Despite inevitable changes, remember: this old friend saw you through awful things long ago, like "post-partum-partum," a unique condition affecting few, where a recent mother (you), having had her baby, rather than get depressed, just forgets she gave birth, gets labor pains again, and hurries to the hospital to deliver—remember, she grabbed you on your way to the hospital again and locked you in your house, thank God!!

Family

Given serial marriage, the Middle-Aged Babe is likely to have serial "ex-husbands" or "husband-like exes," to whom her feelings may run the gamut from "loathes" to "abhors." "Civilized" or "friendly" relationships often sadly follow, as "serial ex-family" may "re-glom onto you." A slew of likable ex-relatives, their offspring, even offspring one raised as one's own (whose father has kept from the Babe for twenty years since), often reappear to glue themselves to the Babe. Results: difficulty with seating arrangements at marriages, remarriages, funerals, graduations, and other "nonfamily family functions."

Sunglasses and Relationships

Sunglasses go a long way toward lubricating such events, should the Babe find herself there—hiding tears, gloating, glee, dismay, fear, a whole carousel of emotions. Sunglasses are therapist-recommended for such times, even at night.

Aging Parents, Far-Flung Siblings, and the Middle-Aged Babe

Boomers away in college leave hometowns, where today, siblings and aging (willful) parents still may be. Thus, a Babe/Siblings issue: "Aging parents." Simple parent dilemmas—totaled cars, lies about taking medicine, "accidentally flushed" tax returns—may be dealt with on the phone. Some much bigger problems, presented below:

Question: "With the savvy of her advanced years, my mom, eighty-one, has decided the sane, appropriate way to cope with shingles is by herself, turning off phones, taking meds 'whenever,' locking out local family, sleeping—and just calling one, lucky, selected sibling who lives a thousand miles away once a day, to say she's alive. To her, this sounds reasonable. How does the far-off Babe cope?"

Question: "A childless great-aunt passes away and her 'Fiddlefern Pattern Sheffield China circa 1680' (ugly, they've spent decades in her attic) suddenly appears on *Antiques Roadshow* with an auction value in the high seven figures. How can the Babe be the one who gets them?"

Question: "An in-house caregiver is seen by friends repeatedly welcoming a pizza man at the door of a Middle-Aged Babe's mom, long on a liquid diet. His delivery truck does 'all-nighters' in the driveway, per a suspicious neighbor who gets her newspaper at 5 a.m. For the Babe, three states away, now what?"

There are no answers to these questions. They just demonstrate the "Chinese Finger Puzzle Nature" of the Middle-Aged Babe's concern with Aging Parents and Nutty Siblings. We see diseases and distances, and the immeasurable cruelty of illness and loss. As soon as this cruelty becomes measurable, we'll produce a second volume, filled with answers. Till then, Babes must forget discount airfares, be ever ready to fly first class, then immediately be introduced to, say a nice hello to, then *scream at* a strange doctor.

Family History/Extended Family History/Serial Marriage Extended Family History

In all cases here, a Babe's motto should be With Charity Toward All and Malice Toward None, but she may perform in the opposite manner. Why? Sunglasses in winter (see above), calming for a short stint at the head table beside your ex-husband and his current wife (the anorexic JCC aerobics instructor) at your daughter's wedding, can help. But such a Babe, stuck at said table *three hours,* might choose (more concealing) *reflective* dark glasses. These allow her more subtly to push her purse down the table, near the detested Babe's-ex-best-friend (hubby's new wife), walk back to her place, then stand, face the crowd, point at the new wife, and yell, "My God, so *that's* where my Judith Leiber bag went!" Grab it, stalk out in front of everybody. *Don't laugh.*

The Middle-Aged Babe Bride: How to Erase a Prenup from His Lawyer's Hard Drive

The single/divorced/widowed Babe knows tons of men. After striking out once or twice in a "fun marriage," she may steer herself toward a new type: the older man, reliable, sane, *there*, engaged in a religion, who may "have things" like "a Vintage IRA," "Serious Assets," "a Vintage 401K," "Bonds," "Interest Income," "Principal to Preserve," or "a Monet." The Babe may enjoy these with him, not hands-on but like quiet classical music that underscores their marriage. Curtailing of that (due to her spouse's sudden passing) plus horror, grief, and unspeakable pain over that loss shouldn't end the angst-quelling "underscoring" to the Babe of his "stuff" (above). His children may object. "Pet charities" or "household staff" may clamor for (or, in his words, "deserve") his possessions, leaving the Babe with little—a few Chopin études. *Despite the Prenup she accidentally signed one day,* having totally forgotten her reading glasses, the Babe, at this nexus of Grief and Stuff, may want some Stuff to quell Grief. Wouldn't you? Thus, the "signing then afterward reading" horrified Babe may wish to adjust the agreement and suddenly want, or be forced to suddenly want, to erase that Prenup from his lawyer's hard drive. How? Easy for the Middle-Aged Babe. Become a regular at the nail salon downstairs from the lawyer, get a pal among the maids on his floor, and learn the lawyer's User ID and Password (from lunching with the lawyer, then watching while he types them to get his e-mail). Thus, any Babe can erase the Prenup totally! Bad behavior? Disgusting! Aghast-at-themselves Babes agree, but if you were in *their* Rockports, might you "go there," too? It's a desperate situation. A possibly marrying Babe can poll her own soul, take a position, or not sign the Prenup to begin with.

Serial Marriage: Though Childless, How to Be a Middle-Aged Babe Grandmother

The older, never married Babe may finally marry, now that men have become old and almost normal. Such men may have children, even grandchildren. First Marriage Babes then find they're endlessly minding an ex-wife's grandchildren (an odd feeling). If they are infants, speak to them only in French (so they learn it and take your orders). Older kids? Use English, which most speak some version of. Some no-nos: chocolate all day, TV all day, and (if they're horrendous) not buying them juice boxes or getting so, so pissed you whisper "fuck you" in their ear when they're sleeping.

Gave Birth? How to Parent a Three-Year-Old *While* Parenting a Twenty-Three-Year-Old (And Look Great Doing It!)

Babes can marry early, marry serially, and, finally, marry a much younger guy with "partial custody" of his kids. This Babe, then, may find herself parenting a three-year-old while parenting her own twenty-three-year-old. If everyone is a girl, good: the Babe has a built-in sitter (her daughter) who, if she has no life, will gladly leave her Swinging Lower East Side Loft every Saturday night to come to Pelham and stare into space for several hours, while the little one jumps on her bed and sings, "If You're Happy and You Know it Clap Your Hands." This gives the Middle-Aged Mom "prep time" to "fluff up," pluck when necessary, and look "fast track hot," like her younger, go-go spouse. Also, there's "accidental peri-menopausal childbearing," with major issues for older moms—questions like: Should babies born by cesarean have horoscopes? And: When are breast pumps right in restaurants? Breast-pumping, gray-haired moms dot Manhattan's Upper West Side, lending a geriatric/lactating, urban *je ne sais quoi* to many New York restaurants!

Old Boyfriends

Babes have skillions, shameless boors who do things like (as one Babe reported) shout, "Of course I look familiar—you slept with me for eight years!" in the middle of Fifty-seventh Street. Old boyfriends are of two categories: Losers and Married (subcategory: Married Losers). If you see one who isn't, with his incredibly-attractive-young-attorney girlfriend, the universal, mandatory drill is:

1. Ask her if she is employed. Ask if she went to Harvard and what her grades were.
2. Call her "fat," but like Gene Wilder called Zero Mostel "fat" in the original movie of *The Producers*: Look at her and yell, "Fat!" Then (pause, yell louder) "Fat, Fat, Fat!"

They'll leave the restaurant.

11. Fat: A Global View
Diet: The Middle-Aged Middle

Can you pinch an inch? How about a foot? Diet defeats fat, and the Middle-Aged Babe knows her enemy's turf. Here, a flabby footsoldier's view of various kinds of fat, principally cellulite.

KEY:
XXX=cellulite deposits visible through new technology!

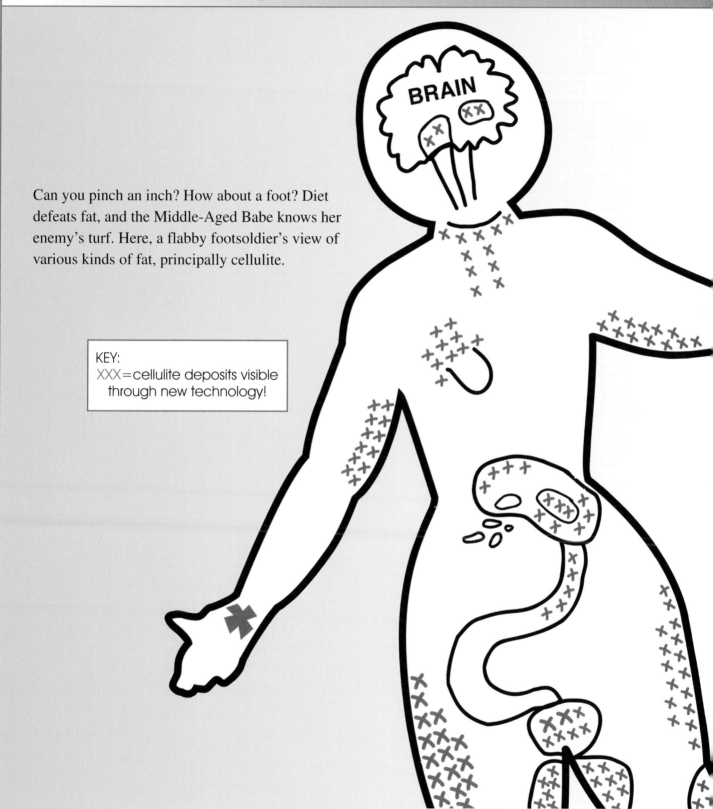

A Complete History of Cellulite

Cellulite (worse than smooth, dangling, hanging, or rippled fat) is the most famous fat. Cellulite, fat in puckered bunches, afflicts everyone in the fat-having community, especially Middle-Aged Babes. Today we know, of course, that cellulite is made of whipped egg whites wrapped lightly in elastic bands, which somehow burrow into and under the skin of the adult female through unregulated body openings. But how do you cope with this "infidel bubble fat" (as it was first known in early Egyptian writings)?

Historically, this most hated and feared fat plagued Philistine Babes, Early Christian Babes, Alexandrite Babes, Jewish Babes, Norman Babes, Moor and Boer Babes. Early pagan civilizations believed cellulite was a cruse from idols that had been broken (and, as revenge, reassembled itself, chip by chip, within the female thigh). Relief was only found by Edwardian, Pilgrim, and other happily overclothed Babes, like Queens and fat Indian Babes in saris. Kimonos and cheongsams mark crude early attempts to cope with "Devil Fat," as it was known in the East (which is why today ducks are hung upside down in Chinatown restaurants—to ward off gods thought responsible for cellulite, hidden in dishes like "Moo Shu Crisco" and "Savory Spicy Pork Rinds," rarely served today).

Changes in This Fat's Landscape

Our century has seen vast changes in the cellulite landscape. Myriad female-written texts dilate upon cellulite; it became a major literary theme among women writers. Little acknowledged in academic circles (now or then), it was first given voice in the writings of Jane Austen, who wrote of cellulite as a "vestigial congenital faux pas," which, she said, "made merry 'neath the gowns of all North England, with small 'coquette briquettes' teasing unflattering billows, like tiny, moored hot-air balloons, into the otherwise slim peplums of all Hertfordshire." Cellulite was later reviled by Edith Wharton, who called it "the plague of the hausfrau visited on the gentry, whose otherwise least galling trait was early morning breath like a carriage horse." Gertrude Stein likened its enlarging effect to the "fascists of Spain, bent on broadening its borders in a cellulitic frenzy"; and Dorothy Parker wrote, "*House Beautiful* is play awful, awful as cellulite." Lillian Hellman, declining to testify in the McCarthy hearings, wrote to a judge, "I cannot cut my conscience to fit the fashion of the time, particularly when that fashion may expand in size at any moment, from New Look Dior svelte to voluminous Lane Bryant, by the cellulite-like widening of the great government lie in which we may, only now, safely fit." The widely bantered sobriquet, "*les pouf globs jambes de fromage de la petite maison*" ("cottage cheese thighs"—Colette), caused a female uproar in Paris, prefiguring the sixties feminist movement (and the scientific advances against cellulite we presently enjoy) (many, sadly, limited to the wealthy, discussed later). Simone de Beauvoir, a rare female champion of "cellulitism," saw cellulite as defining the female body's "evolutionary centrism," confirming nature-intended "female-driven reproduction," and challenging men's significance both in replicating "humans" and, more important, "defining or contributing to the definition of humanness" (these little-known writings occurred *after* Sartre moved out). Susan Sontag, in the same vein, saw "unattractively perceived cellulite" as just another route to the metaphor supporting "quashing of a female-centric culture" and for "female sidelining."

Early Detection

Initially, only royalty were privy to early, alchemy-like cellulite-effacing efforts. Queen Victoria enjoyed a three-day "Dimpled Demon Full Body Plaster" monthly, in the privacy of her dungeon: chloroform, absinthe, and heroin soaked bandages wrapped the royal person to chemically leach cellulite-inducing toxins (figure 1). The patient was then suspended vertically, for liquefying cellulite to drip out of the body onto canvas below mechanism. The two-week-long, torturous "Impossible Squeeze-Leak Fortnight" (its nickname) was endured (here in a rare photo of an unknown royal) but was often entirely ineffective. It was relegated later to a punishment device for political prisoners.

Civil War Doctors Confused

Civil War doctors tripped on "The Blunderbuss of Wonder," a cannon mechanism based on vastly misunderstanding how soldiers in steady, brutal combat lost so much weight (believing fat got "shot off").

Wealthy matrons North and South leaped to stand before this find for "mastery of the stippled hindquarter," popular into the 1920s. The "Blunderbuss of Wonder," generally aimed at the thighs, became a toy of the rich, "played with" recklessly at parties (shown here at an all-night revel in a remote field on a Locust Valley estate, with an alcoholic mistress of Scott Fitzgerald) (figure 2).

It was used with abandon, first in small private clubs run by bootleggers, later by willful heiresses with wide bottoms, in remote areas of estates from Grosse Pointe to Newport (where the subsequent funerals were secretly held). Tragically misunderstood as a party toy, Lost Generation abuse motivated both Ford Madox Ford and Ezra Pound to condemn it in little-known writings; as Pound wrote, "The blunderbuss of failure / foil to those golden fatty female orbs / voluptuous excess, lov'd by men alone? / whose wonders at twilight it catches in its sights to acclaim / rouses, celebrates, adores / later douses / like a lamp which must snuff out its master."

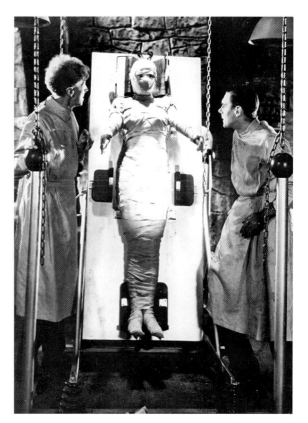

(figure 1)
"Dimpled Demon Full Body Plaster"

(figure 2)
"The Blunderbuss of Wonder"

Great Cellulite Leap Forward Results in the Manhattan Project

The forties brought the "Cellulite Dispersion Master" (figure 3), costly and a touch dangerous, with its retractable breeder reactor, plutonium X-ray "cellulite-zap treatments" (twenty minutes each day), its therapy cone, made of asbestos, its "Curative Asbestos Seed" implantation technique and ingestible asbestos capsules required. Still, it was widely used, adored, and (as Betty Grable's legs attest) it alone among the others was successful! How tragic that, as we all know, production was halted in the early forties, due to the need for radioactive plutonium in the war effort, and its quote-unquote possible "deadly" effects. Research into its stunning early success *did* result in the Manhattan Project.

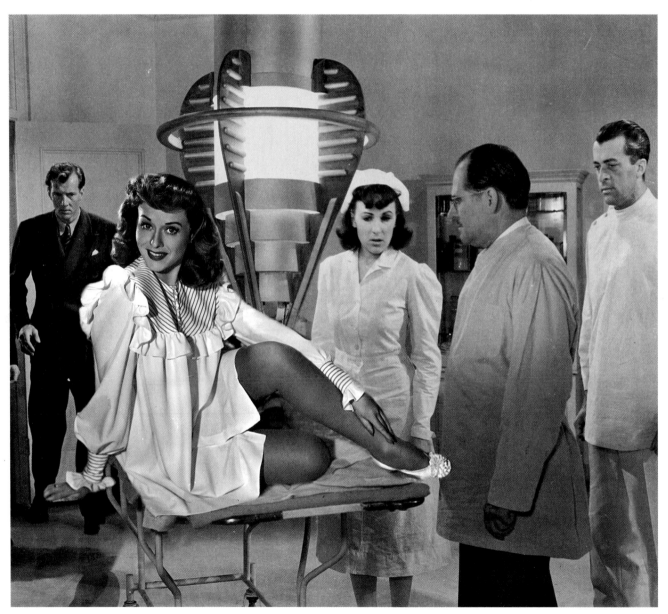

(figure 3)
"Cellulite Dispersion Master"

New "It's Your Fault" Therapy

Sixties psychology's Human Potential Movement greatly influenced "cellulite coping techniques." Cellulite Aversion Group Therapy (figure 4) began in the early sixties—the first psychiatric "talk therapy" to deal with cellulite as a mental problem (as we still know it today). Cellulite Aversion Therapy *then* (in line with dominant psychology of the time) determined this was "people-pleasing fat," "admitted entry" by its bulbous "victim-hosts" to make them "less good" (or "less attractive," thus less threatening to sixties husbands, as sixties women ventured into the workplace for the first time and, as widely

(figure 4)
"Cellulite Aversion Therapy"

feared, into "Go-Go Palaces," chain restaurants, Snack Bars, and God knows where, all alone!). Therapy modalities of the period: subjects were forced to say, "Do I look fat in this? Do I look fat in this?" to each other over and over again for eight or ten hours, or till one client equipped with a "prophylactic butcher knife" screamed, "Not anymore!" and lunged at another; police were called and the session was ended (only to pick up again next morning). Later Babes coped with home remedies, like the anticellulite firming and toning bottom masque (regular or mint, a cucumber slice on each buttock cheek, forty-five minutes a day)—time-consuming, with a short-lived result.

Elitist Method

Weight Watchers used "trickle-down" methods of Cellulite Aversion Therapy with the general populace's smooth but disgusting regular fat (or "A-Cellulite"). Cellulite Aversion Therapy, as many learned the hard way, does not work without all-day daily sessions, inconvenient as women began college and joined the workforce in staggering numbers.

Cellulite "Club Hops"

The seventies held few "cellulite-defying innnovations"; the Cellulite Sciences were indeed "put off" by "Jordache Jeans" (a cellulite-squooshing, masking, girdle-like denim pant), disco's aerobic effect, cocaine, and Studio 54's mandatory "velvet rope cellulite check," when (legend has it) Steve Rubell himself was turned away.

Scientific Advances

Current scientific advances hold much promise, as internal scanning devices have led to "mapping" the human cellulite "genome deposit route." Scientists at the San Diego company Intellulite have identified and labeled more than 1,200 "Human Cellulitic Sites," which they may now find, but not fix, in patients in a two- to five-hour scanning process (costing more than sixteen thousand dollars, and held only in San Diego: still, wildly popular).

During the Sixties' "British Invasion," scantily clad Go-Go Dancers in raised Go-Go Cages were squeamish about "visibly shaking cellulite" when ponying before tony, leering crowds at Go-Go Clubs.

Dance doesn't undo cellulite (even on the thinnest Go-Go-Booted Babe thigh). Thus, a small UK firm ("The Mod Bod, Inc.") devised the "Post-Buga-loo Sweat Box" where a hot air surge from twenty-four welded-in, hand-held hairdryers (then new, all the rage) was thought to pierce, explode cellulite globules at their most vulnerable—just post-dance, when muscles, cellulite were warm, malleable. The "Hullabaloo Hell Hole" (dubbed by users, a fixture at many clubs), however, failed, as heating the sweaty body after hours of painful ponying was unbearable; the machine was both despised and, as later discovered, entirely ineffective, a deadly combo for any new product. The firm refitted boxes to treat upper arm cellulite, but the "Do the Jerk, Baby, Do the Jerk Now Box" (same mechanics: welded-in hairdryers set higher up) also failed. Machine scrap metal was sold to build the first prototypes of planes with upstairs bars, and to construct faux, black-market Les Paul guitars (said to be favored by the Beatles).

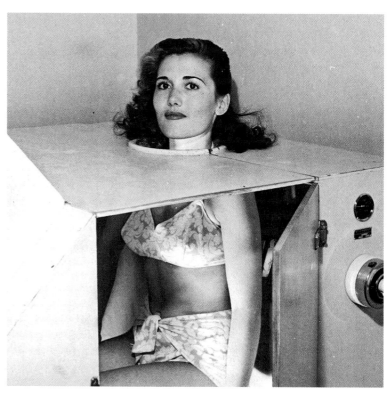

(figure 5) "Cellulite Sweat Box"

Intellulite identified cellulite as "smart fat" (which seeks the approval of authority figures and machines, two things it can't differentiate between, thus racing up to the scan apparatus for better detection). Printouts of scans, still crude, are first reviewed by doctors on a screen *during* the Intellulite scan (figure 6), allowing a directed examination of elusive "Duodenal Cellulititis," "Bipolar cellulombosis," and "Upper Thigh Sub-dural Suet Balloon Bags (bilateral)" (or "saddlebags"). These areas hold out the most promise for treatment (currently there is no treatment, except for the "Upper Thigh Subdural Suet Balloon Bags"—bilateral or not—which respond to liposuction. Sadly, the others can only be studied and identified.

"Most baffling," says Dr. Avi Borgs-Christensen, "is why some cells turn into cellulite, and some do not. We are perplexed by 'Rear flank catwalk quiver' and 'Thigh udders,' which seem somehow geneti-cally based but impervious to early detection or to preventive inter-utero injections before the birth of a female child (injections we *have* developed). As well, we believe 'Intra-thigh bicoastal flabial units in the lower quadrant' may have something critical to do with childbearing and should not necessarily be considered for demolition." (See figure 7.)

Concern also exists about "Carpal tunnel metaglobs" (a rare cellulite of the hand, the by-product of non–computer use), and, critically, recently found in the brain, 'Amygdala cellulata' and 'Hippocampus cellulititis,' thought to impede the college admissions process. 'Bladder cellulite congestive disorder,' 'Tracheal cellulite,' and 'Cardiac cellulotosis' are also matters for concern (blockages may develop, and the look of low-cut gowns affected). These worrisome fat-related disorders can be discovered but for the moment only stared at.*

---

* and only in San Diego

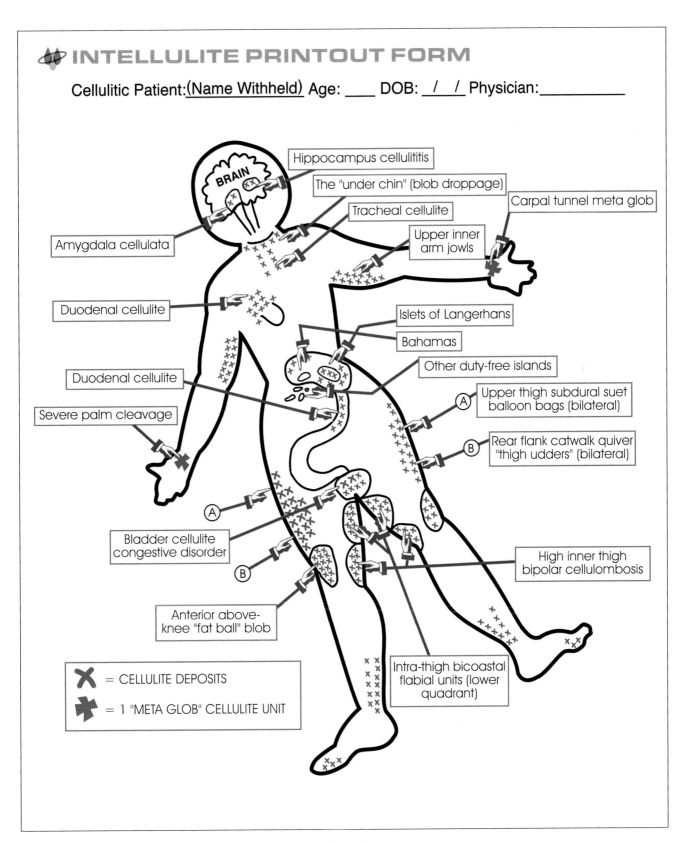

(figure 6)
Intellulite Printout of simple cellulite scan with diagnostic markings

(figure 7)
Here, Dr. Borgs-Christensen precision-lights a patient to be scanned for never-before detectable inner-body cellulite pockets, undiscoverable in an ordinary visual or manual cellulite examination. These are known as interior "Cellulite Repository Sites" and can be crucial for good cardiac health and jumping about in a two-piece bathing suit without children laughing.

Wonders of Research

Intellulite, having produced the first "Intellulite Scan" (a cellulite diagnostic tool) has also made its first Cellulite Reducing Bombardment Device (which can be used at home, but only if an additional room is built onto the house for the equipment, and an adjacent room built for cooling equipment for the equipment in the first room). Cellulite, as Intellulite foresees, will be bombarded forty-five minutes a day, with "secret particles," sufficient to cause implosion permanently within a year, maybe. If (as research has shown) it inevitably reappears (in a month or less), a "post-bombardment bombardment" will be required forty-five minutes twice a day using more "secret particles," and the presence of large, beefy marines near the screen (as mentioned, cellulite is a "smart fat," though unable to tell the difference between authority figures and scientific apparatus. Cellulite (principally single, rarely dating molecules), seeing Military Hunks, will swarm to the subject's feet and plunge out through the toenails, glomming onto the men (it's hard to meet guys when you live in someone's thighs). Thus, they will simply leave the person's person permanently (process still being developed).

Only Certain Architects

Only certain architects are licensed to design such homes. They can be built only on specific terrain (ample land, municipalities with flexible building regulations and easy architecture review boards). For some, bombardment devices *for every part of the body* may soon be built, housed, and cooled the moment they're invented; others will find a sad paucity of such equipment. A lack of power supply support facilities may exist, as well as power, affecting the U.S. real estate market, as "flush neighborhoods" impinge on nearby, less tony, power-line-rich ones.

Following: plans (showing additional acreage for current and projected bombardment suites) for a new home designed for this purpose in Bel Air, California.

Hope for the Future

The "de rigueur" Bel Air Anticellulite Home eludes most Babe budgets. But there's *still hope* for those of us who aren't movie stars, which is unusual.

Architect's Rendering: Residence of (Hollywood Movie Star, Name Withheld)
(with existing and projected cellulite bombardment suites)

5 Projected design plans (on adjacent acres) for future, full-body and other cellulite bombardment suites when invented.

Cooling Unit

1 Upper subdural suet balloon bags, bilateral vacuum Cooling Unit

2 Bipolar cellulombosis locator

3 Duodenal cellulite extractor

4 Tracheal cellulite suction

Architect: Zoe Schmoe   Date:

Client: (Name Withheld)   Address: 12364 Bellagio Way

Leaps Forward

Today, some real leaps forward: Cellulite Aversion Therapy groups thrive, with local chapters, self-help Cellulite Support Groups promoting worldwide understanding of cellulite as a disease. There are twenty-four-hour emergency cellulite phone banks, and one-on-one "cellulite buddy" support. Groups, and their websites, follow.

Cellulite Support Groups

"Antelope Reservoir Moms Against Skirted Swimsuits"
www.CelluliteinMontana.org

"Never Say 'Cottage Cheese Thighs' of Rome, New York"
www.Droop\chin.org

"Never Say 'Cottage Cheese Thighs' of Pretoria, South Africa"
www.Size5\Soon.S.A.org

"Jamais dit 'Poufs globs de fromage de la petite maison des jambes,' d' Avignon, France"
www.Jamaispoufsglobs\surlepontd'Avignon.org

"Hope is in the Lord, Our Slimmed Down Higher Power"
www.OutofControlRearEndsofGreaterCincinnati.org

"Disgruntled Ex-Drum Majorettes of Dallas/Fort Worth"
www.Disgrun\blobbyhotties.org

In California: "The Fatted Calif"
www.fattedcalifptui.com

"Friends with Saddlebags: We Are Hartford's Soft Underbelly"
www.NewEnglandRegionalSoftUnderbelly.com

"Upper-Inner-Arm Jowls in Poughkeepsie: A Way Out"
www.UpperInner\Please!.org

"The Bulbous, Pitted Underchins of Xtapa"
www.Blobbing_out_so_Glommingontoeachother\Xtapa.org

Diet, then, greatly concerns the Middle-Aged Babe. Here we will examine two revolutionary (fast and *so easy!*), never-before-revealed diet options. We begin with:

Sample Diet One

The Middle-Aged Babe's Babe-in-a-Minute Minute-Meltdown Diet

The Middle-Aged Babe's Babe-in-a-Minute Minute-Meltdown Diet, unlike other diets, which require eight glasses of water a day, speeds the process by requiring eighty glasses of water a day for a far faster result, if one subtracts time for trips to the bathroom and adds it to number of pounds lost!

Wildly effective, this diet lists an array of *varied* tasty waters. And The Babe-in-a-Minute Minute-Meltdown Diet denotes exactly *when* to drink the eighty glasses of water, to fit in all eighty.

Here, wonderful variations keep this diet interesting!

The Middle-Aged Babe's Babe-in-a-Minute Minute-Meltdown Diet

Water Menu for Week One

12 MIDNIGHT	water (six glasses) w/sedative of choice
1 A.M.	water (three glasses)
2 A.M.	water (ten glasses)
3 A.M.–6 A.M.	sleep (strapped to waterproof mattress)
7 A.M.	newspapers, elimination, "wake-up water" (with caffeine additive) (twelve glasses)
8 A.M.	CNN, exercise, water (three glasses), elimination, exercise, water (two glasses), exercise
9 A.M.	water (fifteen glasses) / exercise (load bearing)
10 A.M.–12 NOON	elimination (conduct law practice from bathroom)
12 NOON	water (three glasses)
1:15 P.M.	water (one glass)
2:30 P.M.	water (four flagons)
3:01 P.M.	water (three glasses/two glasses—choice)
4 P.M.	water (one tumbler)
5 P.M.	water (one cocktail glass)
6 P.M.	water (small pitcher)
7 P.M.	water (four tankards)
8 P.M.	water aperitif, water straight up, water chaser
9 P.M.	water "hot toddy" (one goblet)
10 P.M.	bath; drink it immediately after
11 P.M.	water (six chalices)

Repeat for seven days.

With such easy recipes, and a potential to lose 7 to 50 pounds per week,* this diet is a must-do for the driven Middle-Aged Babe.

---

* Includes minutes spent in bathroom added to total pounds lost.

Sample Diet Two

The Middle-Aged Babe's Food Aversion Diet

The Middle-Aged Babe sees many diets that require food purchase from the Diet Program. Many include counseling and weigh-ins, but their food, tasty, "gourmet-chef prepared," and costly, once gone, must be replaced—an expensive add-on given the membership fee, *and* a diet that continues for weeks and months (even while "plateauing," when Babes are stuck at one weight for some time).

The Middle-Aged Babe's Food Aversion Diet requires the dieter to buy food *only once,* prepared at a central weighing station/gourmet kitchen, in weekly portions, from Cordon Bleu–type recipes replete with cream and butter, "no-no's" for most Babe diets. This diet permits savory entrees and fab desserts like the Middle-Aged Babe's Food Aversion Diet Chocolate Blackout Torte, with fudge-filled strawberries. What's different? First, how food is presented (presentation, *critical!*); second, how it's ingested (or not). Here, two desserts "pre-presentation": first, the Middle-Aged Babe's Food Aversion Diet Chocolate Blackout Torte before serving.

Looks luscious, no? Now, *presentation* of the dessert, as the Middle-Aged Babe, served, lifts her fork for a first bite:

See, isn't presentation *all*? Here, it *prevents weight gain* as Babe is unable (and terrified, unwilling, *even* if she'll stay in room) to ingest this, with a loss of 500 to 1,000 calories! (And add "aerobic fear fat burn" as Babe panics, races out, screaming, thus shedding additional pounds!)

Here's a French favorite: dark chocolate poured and chilled lavishly, atop a dense, strawberry-dotted cheesecake, rich as cream. Equally tempting! Now, we'll go to the moment of presentation, as the Babe inserts her fork, to prod:

Instant weight loss via precisely timed presentation and attempted ingestion! The terrified, svelte Babe can expect to be served "seconds," repeatedly, for days, because after serving, the dish "returns to normal," may be quiet, docile, even nap while refrigerated, but whenever it is served, attacks and attacks again, night after night, till goal weight is reached! *What a diet!*

Rather than more "sample diets" (Babes have plenty), some oft-asked Diet Questions:

Q&A

Q: What can I eat nonstop that won't affect my weight? *You have to tell me.*

A: Paper, lemons, Kleenex. These are the big three that naturally come to mind. Or, for a great treat, unflavored gelatin from Herb-Ox, heated, cooled, tinted with blue food coloring, then frozen in ice cube trays and sucked on a toothpick. Another treat? Cellophane noodles, ordered from a Chinese restaurant, covered with Sweet'n Low and rolled, by hand, into little Dunkin' Donuts balls—"cellophane munchkins."

Q: What is (or isn't) "water weight"?

A: Everything is water weight.

Q: I'm a career woman *and* full-time mom with pressures—sometimes I go crazy bingeing! Crazy! I end up buying a box of donuts, then running water on them before I can finish them. Also, buying chocolate bars, then flushing them down the toilet before finished, or setting fire to boxes of Oreos before I even open them! Help! What are some plain "good sense" things I can do to control my eating?

A: Actually, unfortunately, and it's with mixed feelings we tell you this—it appears you have hit on them all. Additionally: Sit quietly, no children, work, or other distractions, bend your head forward, close your eyes, and rethink your concept of "plain good sense."

Q: Why are you doing this to me?

A: What? What am I doing to you? Making you go on a diet? I'm not doing that to you! The culture is doing that to you! Geez! Lighten up!

Q: No!

12. Health and the Middle-Aged Babe

Medical great leaps forward have made huge gobs of Health available today that weren't imaginable in centuries past. Drug therapies, diagnostic tools, early detection, and genetic markers promote well-being in millions. Medicine's reach into human "bone and viscera," however, has not gone into the human psyche. Thus, once delighted Babes who discover they just "keep living and living" become dismayed. The "Babe Head" must wrap itself around Medicine's widening parameters (among Medicine's big achievements—"Middle-Aged Babe Technology"—which actually led to the creation of today's fabulous "Middle-Aged Babe") (see Appendix H).

Still, in spite of her "scads of well-being," the Babe gets confused, wondering, "How old am I really?" and (re: Life) "Where now is 'the middle'?" Today's "Drowned in Well-Being Babe," not knowing who, what, how sexy, how old, how young, how pumped up or virtually crippled, how ready for complete-overhaul-plastic-surgery or way, way late for it she is, is *so majorly turned around.* As well, medicine's whimsical, new "inconclusive pathology" reports require that Babes must accept, in the future, hideous things no one knows will ever really happen to them, and are assured, often right before they *do* happen, that they absolutely won't, till, just now, when they do. When in high school did we learn how to handle this? The "I'd Just as Soon Not Know Babe" (discontinued model; being re-readied for market) "deflects" Medicine's "way, way too much information"—Medicine only "faintly foresees" cures for stuff it now has precise diagnostic tests for! A real "medical mind fuck" for the Middle-Aged Babe! Does Medicine expect to be popular and well-liked for this? Does Medicine want friends? So why does It put the Babe in this Medical Cul-de-Sac? And not tell her how to get out?

As automotive speed is measured in "horsepower," so today's medical speed might be measured in "cossack power." That is: a ratio of today's "Jewish Babes" weighed against "those otherwise lost in pogroms, were there cossacks" is great (for Today's Babe). But Medicine hasn't offered Babes clear social roles, as in, for example, cossack-centric *Fiddler on the Roof,* to define her. Is she young, is she old, is she the mother, the daughter, the Matchmaker (Yenta), or the shrieking Dead Butcher's wife who has the big number in Act I? *Fiddler on the Roof* (not often used as a medical tool) suggests: Babes forge new roles themselves, absent today, as we live longer than we were acculturated to. Babes need new *Fiddler on the Roof*–ish "traditions," "cultural niches" the New Babe can fall into, must "culturally self-start," to define her. (Sad note: till recently Middle-Aged Babes in our culture were considered "invisible"—in Hollywood, Middle-Aged Babe-Actresses still are. How, when there are so many Like Babes in the audience, and Babe-Actresses are all still alive, being worked on, in Pacific Palisades, or seen eating at Nate'n Al in Beverly Hills, while firing their agents? And Goldie Hawn looks younger than Kate Hudson! This baffling conundrum confounds Hot-Women Experts globally!

Health Tips for Babes

Today's Babe must cope with what she can't: "inconclusive" MRIs, "abnormal" needle biopsies—murky, major info she copes with, but can't, thus needs some "health tip rules" to keep her from dank psychological waters.

Rule #1: Don't talk about it. If you talk, speculate, jerk yourself around, or moon about, re: any concern, concern grows. So don't. Really.

Rule #2: Don't ask about it. Every disease is different, even with the same names, only in different people. An interesting trait of disease also is that, if announced, in even the most offhand way, everyone will know someone who had it, died of it, or was in such pain from it that it required a Sam's Club Sized Dose of painkillers, administered on a Sam's Club pallet, in Sam's Club, "even to touch the agony." People get off on this discussion. *Don't ask.*

Rule #3: Self-Diagnosis. Babes with time on their hands who watch TV commercials with cheery "Prescription Medicine Songs" sung over quickly announced lists of gruesome symptoms, some of which Babes think they have, develop special "Television Disorders."

Our advice: avoid tabloid or magazine articles (particularly in the genuinely knowledgeable *The Sun* and *The Star*) describing symptoms. Also—count up how many symptoms (in the prescription drug commercial whose theme song you like most) that you think you have. Divide by two. If the answer is one or more, see a doctor. If the answer is one or less, see a doctor.

Second Opinions

Some Babes see "second opinions" as insults to their doctor, who is "nice." The Nice Doctor could care less: he gets paid. A "second opinion" either confirms the first, or motivates a third. As well, "Nice," in a doctor, shouldn't be equated with "good." "Revered," "Board-Certified," "Celebrated," "Worshipped," "Famous," or (a preemptive "buy") "Often on *The Today Show*," OK. Lose "nice."

Nice Surgeons

Nobody sane would go to a nice surgeon, as good surgeons rarely are "nice." Generally, the more conceited, obnoxious, and time-pressed and the more obvious users of hairspray surgeons are, the better they are. They are the "Glamour Flyboys" of the Medical Fleet: Big Egos make for great results, including you not dying on the operating table.

Also, re: "second opinions": Don't get them from (above) TV ads for prescription drugs, from "your own personal vibes," "your friends' vibes," your sister, your husband, or someone you ask on the elevator. They should come from a doctor who went to medical school and is board-certified, with your problem as his or her specialty.

The Middle-Aged Babe's Guide to Terrifying New Medical Tests

The Medically Happening Babe is an amateur doctor herself, due to ardent medical reading (in *The New York Times* Health and Science Section, *USA Today,* and United Airlines' *Hemispheres* magazine). The Middle-Aged Babe Standard State—always eager not to die while constantly waiting to get thin—makes her very into such publications, hip to every new, swinging test. Here, a partial list of Babe Favorite, Hyper-New, Terrifying Upcoming Medical Tests (assuming they get approved by the FDA).

1. **The Brain Smear.** Baby Wipes on the ends of Bic pens inserted orthoscopically (like a mini-cam in knee surgery) through the ear, swab brain cells to diagnose (or cause—a minor drawback in the FDA's view) migraines, "swelled head," or "attitude tumors" (psychologically induced growths).

2. **Intrapupil Probe.** Simultaneous exam of both eyes, with drops, loved by Babes as it rarely results in a script for "unblended bifocals."

3. **Colovagiscope.** A combo colon/vaginal probe, like the "lunar probe," miniaturized. The doctor observes little men climbing into or between the colon and vaginal areas, possibly having to climb over suspected "obstructions" or blockages to get there. Such setbacks, recorded on the motion picture "scope," allows the "colovagiscopologist" to review tests very precisely later (and edit out scenes he doesn't like).

4. **Otolaryngalathon.** Forty-eight-hour input through vocal cords, into ears, during which the Babe's voice, like a preprogrammed Hammond organ, sings endless "Best-Loved American Standards" on headsets into the Babe's own ears, which react or not; measures hearing and possible future singing carreer.

5. **The Cleavogram.** Mammogram of oft-missed "breastal crease," "breastal valley," or "cleavage."

6. **Digital Capillary Dilation.** A punch in the eye by an ophthalmologist enlarges and better exposes distorted blood flow pattern to socket and also aids doctor immensely in getting your bill paid on time (if performed often enough).

7. **Mammo Press 'n' Squeeze.** A step beyond mammogram, this painful procedure produces astonishingly clear, thorough results.

8. **Vaginal Flush 'n' Lube.** Self-explanatory.

How the Middle-Aged Babe Interprets Results of Medical Tests

Having been examined by "the best Heart Surgeon in the world," or "the best Ear, Nose, and Throat Specialist in the world," and had tests, patients often panic when they get results, even Babes amply equipped with pens, papers, questions, and relatives. They're often confused as to what results mean. Doctors, who obfuscate bad news unless asked direct questions, don't elaborate.

The Middle-Aged Babe, with her endlessly optimistic nature, realizes—it doesn't matter what the results *exactly mean,* but rather, if they are good or bad. Here, then, is "The Official Middle-Aged Babe's Guide to Medical Test Results and Their Interpretation."

Negative	good		Viral	good
Positive	good if you want		Borderline	very good
	to get pregnant		Slightly elevated	good
Inconclusive	probably good		Mild discoloration	good
Benign	good		Congenital	good
Normal	good		Self-limiting	fabulous
High/Normal	good		Low-grade	good
Low/Normal	good		Advanced	good
Within the normal range	good		Stable	good
Just outside the normal range	good		Degenerative change	probably good
Punctured	very good		Significant deficiency	very good
Stage One	good		Some feeling may return	good
Some limited mobility	good			

Advances unexplored here, but great to glean tons about (available from magazines like *Lancet* or *Hemispheres*): "The Middle-Aged Babe's Home Biopsy and How-to-Read Kit" (from *The New England Journal of Medicine*); "Another View of Internal Bleeding," (*Hemispheres*); "Breast Health and Their Attitude: Related?" (from Southwest Airlines' *Spirit* magazine); and, for pregnant Babes with far-flung families, "What About the Sonogram Simulcast?" (using conference room screens in Kinko's).

Babe Mental Health

Few Mental Health advances, save psychopharmacology, assist the Middle-Aged Babe. This is in part due to the crash of "Talk Therapy." "Talk Therapy," once the "Hermès Birkin Bag of Psychiatry," took a hit and was left pretty much "dead in the water" by the real life of Woody Allen (whether his orgasms are "right on the money" or not). (One imagines Freud, Jung, and Adler crouched in a corner of heaven, waiting to jump Woody Allen the minute he shows up.) Still, there's the all-new Ten-Minute Nervous Breakdown" (for the Babe who's talking aloud to her dead husband but has to get to work). Others are:

Special-Occasion Therapy (self-explanatory)
New Uses for "Hope"
Botox for the Soul—coming soon

13. The Middle-Aged Babe's Guide to Conception, Fertility, Menopause, and Contraception

Contraception (or "the opposite of conception") is clearly the Babe's job in our more-than-half Babe, in fact, Babe-top-heavy world. For Babes are, happily, the "conceivors," men merely the "semen placement facilitators" or "jizz dispensation auxiliary technicians." This excludes the increasingly popular "hands-on New Dad," parenting left and right, splitting sleep deprivation, changing diapers, crying openly, while singing, "Kathy's Mom's Got It Goin' On." This Dad, a kind of butch, in-house nanny, is not just a "Conception Extra" as his father's generation was. Still, a warning: *When not parenting aggressively, he may attempt to cause more children.* (See "Contraception" later in this chapter.)

We will also look at "The Middle-Aged Babe's Guide to Fertility and Childbearing" in later sections—the "A Little Late in the Day Mom: Going Direct from In Vitro to Menopause," and the "Fortyish Mom, with Same-Aged Children by Marriage." But first, brief looks at "Little-Known Causes of Infertility" and "Menopause."

Conception and Infertility

Earlier in life, the Babe faced many issues regarding contraception. Then, she might have hoped for barrenness ("hope," an iffy mode of contraception). Barrenness, an inability (or unwillingness?) to conceive, is also unreliable.

The "will to be barren," however strong, will often fail, as cited in literature and film: Endless examples include, notably: *A Summer Place, Gone with the Wind,* the Book of Genesis, *The Life of Sally Hemmings, Tarzan and Jane Find a Son, The Best of Everything, Anna Karenina* (see Reading List, Appendix I, single-spaced, last 250 pages). The inability to conceive is welcome among the "Menopausal Yet a Sexual Beehive of Activity" Babes, but loathed among Babes in the categories "Dying to Reproduce," "Hell-Bent to Reproduce," and "So Desperate They Will Pay Strangers to Reproduce for Them." Many Babes' child-having crusades will lead them to ingest vats of drugs.[*] Strong "offspring cravings" alternatively drive them to places like China or Poland to pick up a baby, then fly right back to parent it, parenting wildly, just parenting left and right, not even stopping for five days in Paris to buy clothes, or to stroll through Venice leaving the baby with the concierge at the Gritti Palace, *nothing.* And they could get a triangle fare! What is this "flying straight from Shanghai, compulsively parenting, not even pausing in Hong Kong to 'get some fabulous high-definition TV equipment and have some "Chanel" suits made'" madness about?

---

[*] Then they will go to doctors and take fertility drugs.

Some Reasons for Conception Difficulty

Infertility

The days are long gone when sex and conception were one. Now they are separate, a Process from which children may or may not arise. For whatever reason, children do not simply come forth, rat-a-tat, creating a lovely continent like China, as they once did. Here, how the Middle-Aged Babe may cope.

Little Known Causes

While the conception-strapped Babe learns much from doctors, there are little-known, under-researched causes of infertility doctors miss, which the alert Babe must know exist anecdotally, and we will reveal here, some for the first time. These all-new possible infertility causes include:

1. **"Ricochet Ejaculation"**—During intercourse, semen "bounces back" or "leaps out" of the vagina and back into the penis. Dangerous to passersby, "ricochet ejaculation" is due to the angle of penetration, the attitude of the penetrator or of the sperm (which may be hyper, "joking around," or simply, having been shot out of there like a bat out of hell, terrified).
2. **"Pelvic ADD"** (Pelvic Attention Deficit Disorder)—An antsy pelvis, bored and hyper, fidgets during intercourse, or talks to its neighbor, or runs around the room screaming the names of all the characters on *South Park* and simply can't pay enough attention to release an egg and have it fertilized. It may be a delightful, otherwise perfectly normal, bright pelvis except for this problem, which can be treated with Pelvic Ritalin, causing the pelvis to cool out, veg, and conceive.

    Less common:

1. **"Penile Attention Deficit Disorder"**—An unruly, headstrong penis engaged in sex becomes erect, then suddenly completely loses interest and wanders off to learn if you can see Venus from the dining room window or to read comic books. (*Note:* Occasionally—rarely—both conditions, "Pelvic ADD" and "Penile ADD," exist at the same time. (See "Adoption.")
2. **"Inverted Vagina"**—The vaginal opening occurs in the interior of the body, causing "menstruating up," and some other minor problems with sex, conception, and birth.
3. **"Sperm Interns"**—To cut costs, a man may have few real sperm and taken on too many unpaid "sperm interns," not prepared or trained sufficiently to do a professional job.
4. **"Ovarian Flatulence"**—A buildup of gas in the ovaries simply offends the semen, causing them to turn back or politely excuse themselves. Also causes bloating in women who fail to get into jeans in department stores that "were always their size before."
5. **"Ovulatory Ambivalence"**—The "ambivalent ovary" often occurs in Younger Middle-Aged Career Babes, whose brain is not sending a clear signal to the ovaries about whether they really want to get pregnant. The "I can go either way" ovary is not a help in fertility; also known as "Passive-Aggressive Ovary Disorder."
6. **"Vaginal Reflux"**—Causes the semen to "back up" in the vagina, resulting in "vagina burn," a "churning vagina," an acidic womb, or a baby who loves Mylanta.

Coping with Fertility "Dismay"

The Middle-Aged Babe and her partner may be "greatly dismayed" (or "hysterical") by her inability to conceive. "Vintage ovum" may be the problem (in Older Middle-Aged Babes). Or, in Much, Much Older Middle-Aged Babes, "Totally retro ova" (can be diagnosed on a sonogram!). Ovaries appear, on the sonogram, to be shaped like Roseville pottery, 1950s car fins, or anything from the Andy Warhol sale at Sotheby's, and are just too old (or, as they are medically known, "kitsch") to produce eggs.

Raising the Intrauterine Mood

The wise Babe knows *her* mood *and* her intrauterine mood are critical to fertility. She knows to cheer up, even elevate the mood of the uterus. How? Paxil, Wellbutrin, and other "mood elevators" are ineffective inserted vaginally (at this time).

Babes can beef up the dispirited uterus through other means. Decorating the uterus with comfy, inviting furniture or other festive elements like "All Sperm Welcome" banners, or gaily colored douches (a regular douche solution, mixed with several Rit dyes and glitter), to start. Babes raise uterine spirits by giving the uterus presents (shot in through tampons) or throwing the uterus small parties it can attend laparoscopically, held in hospital operating rooms the Babe rents and caters for the day (with the laparoscope inserted backward, the camera part facing the party, so the whole event can be shown to the uterus, and taped for future viewing, to lift its mood again and again). A dispirited uterus is no friend to conception. Also, the man's fertility must also be tested. A sperm count should be ordered and, if necessary, followed up by a "Sperm Audit," done by Price Waterhouse/Bristol-Myers Squibb.

Menopause: An Introduction

One reason for infertility may be the onset of menopause. Sadly, this is often seen in today's new, reproductive-happy Middle-Aged Babe, who tries to push the conception envelope into Late Middle Age, geriatric years, during and after retirement, and even posthumously. But whatever her conception status, the Middle-Aged Babe is fine: whether using contraception, trying to get pregnant, going through menopause, or, as is often the case today, doing all three at the same time.

Entirely Unknown Till the Present

Nothing was known about menopause, nor was it mentioned aloud, until, like, *just now,* when members of the Baby Boom began to spontaneously combust into it. Before, it seemed to be some wacky fakey nightmare-thing that happened to someone (an illustration) in a High School Health Book (not even to our mothers, who never mentioned it), just *someone* incredibly old, somewhere, who wouldn't mind having it and was barely breathing anyway, indeed a stranger near death (note third syllable, *"pause"*). Menopause seemed butted right up *against* death, like two stores in a shopping center. The shopping center of death.

Disbelief

Now it's happening to the Baby Boom, the very people who *invented youth! We* are aging, *we,* who thought up everything young and cool! Bell-bottom jeans, premarital sex, every cool idea, ours!! We invented rock music, pass-fail, Give Peace a Chance, saying "fuck," rock divas, serial marriage, snowboarding, living together! *We* invented ordering in, "getting high," Monday holidays, George Harrison, garlic mashed potatoes—*and* we invented the long self-indulgent harangue where people just go on and on about themselves forever—God, don't we deserve something for that, like getting out of menopause entirely—but, oh, no, it is we, incredibly, *we, who are pausing in our meno!* Not that anyone was so grooving on having their period, *but please! As if we aged!* Seriously, would you like to know how we age? I'll tell you how the Baby Boomer ages: BY STAYING YOUNG!! AND DON'T GIVE US ANY *SHIT* ABOUT THIS, I DON'T CARE IF I'M IN MENOPAUSE OR NOT, WE'RE NOT OLD, *WE ARE YOUNG PEOPLE WHOSE AGE JUST HAPPENS TO BE HIGH!!* A clerical glitch. And is Twiggy having menopause, or Ike and Tina Turner? Can we e-mail them and find out, because I'm not doing this with just Lauren Hutton. Seriously!

Theoretical Issues: *Fin*

Those, then, are the theoretical issues surrounding menopause. Now, the practical issues. First, what causes menopause? Clearly, running out of blood. Estrogen levels decline, and the blood just quits being in the "blood place" adjacent to the uterus. Lowered estrogen levels induce the start of "perimenopause," a pre-menopausal state named after Perry Como, when the woman experiences body and mood changes, becomes more mellow, and swinging, with a beautiful baritone, starts wearing sweaters with three buttons and patches on the elbows and starring on her own network TV series. Still, perimenopause can be a beautiful time, probably.

What Is Estrogen?

Estrogen is a powerful if vengeful hormone affecting a woman's fertility, moods, sleep patterns, appetite. Estrogen is the household heating oil of womanhood. Much has been learned about it—Estrogen comes in many forms: gel, mint gel, paste (mint or regular), and the Pump.

Estrogen is made in a toothpaste factory. How does it work? To put a very technical process into layman's terms, Estrogen puts up an invisible wall like "Gardol," which keeps you from turning into a guy. As Estrogen declines, and perimenopause starts, symptoms begin. Differentiated from menstrual symptoms, which include depression, anxiety, PMS, mood swings, and weight swings, the new perimenopause symptoms include depression, anxiety, PMS-*like* mood swings, and weight swings. The difference? During menstruation, the symptoms occur only three weeks out of the month; in perimenopause, they occur four weeks out of the month.

Let's examine the true Middle-Aged Babe's correct reaction to menopause, symptom by symptom.

Hot Flashes

A powerful emotional "leveler," Estrogen maintains calm, a sense of well-being. It informs moments of happiness, elation. When it is "revoked," these emotions (like people on *Supermarket Sweep* let loose in

Bulgari) go crazy: happiness, sadness, depression race around "Bulgari," crashing their shopping carts into cases full of canary diamonds (your "well-being") and at each other, shattering all. The heat let off by these "crashing" emotions is what causes "hot flashes," sudden floods of "indoor heat" the body flares with—not the precipitous fall in estrogen, as scientists once thought, but a "shopping cart–type scuffle" of the emotions in the Bulgari-like calm of your stomach. That's what one new theory says. Most hold to the older, tried and true idea of what causes hot flashes: men.

And what is a hot flash? It is as if your skin were a cigarette, and your whole body suddenly asked for a light. As if your soul were a lightbulb, and Con Ed used the whole Indian Point power plant to turn it on for a joke. As if, during a perfectly normal lunch, you suddenly bloom with heat because the Zambelli Brothers just set off one of those big, trembling, "sky-filling" fireworks from the Macy's July Fourth celebration within your Versace suit, for practice.

Yet Babehood thrives throughout menopause, dragging womanhood along with it. Even the sudden hot flash—relaxing in a chair, having your hair cut, while spontaneously combusting with the body heat of someone eating Indian food while sitting on a space heater—that's *nothing* to the Middle-Aged Babe. Why? Because the Babe has lived an *actual, real life* with all the luxury amenities—death, divorce, AIDS, cancer—which, angst-wise, make menopause seem as big as lost luggage. Indeed, where lesser women may react, the Middle-Aged Babe is too cool, chic, fucked over, and battle scarred even to *notice* menopause (except for a one-second visit to the doctor for symptom relief, as the TV ad with Lauren Hutton suggested).

The Middle-Aged Babe Mom: Direct from In Vitro to Menopause, a "How To"

This sudden change "rocks the world" of Middle-Aged Babes who, having just been pregnant, are suddenly in menopause, causing the Inappropriately Shouting Mom, the Hot Though Making Snowmen Mom, and other anomalies.

The Middle-Aged Babe *so totally doesn't mind, in fact, is delighted with, even titillated by* menopause, as she knows it means sex without pregnancy, skin without zits, beauty without the beast of the period!

Also, new medications abound, and we can share exciting therapies the Middle-Aged Babe may benefit from, previously unknown. These "Hot Flash Great Leaps Forward" (unused before, except in clinical trials) should be available to the Middle-Aged Babe soon, seen here for the very first time.

These new modes enable the ever fabulous Middle-Aged Babe to laugh in hot flashes' faces and continue in her fabulousness.

Hot Flash Advances

The Babe in a low, bias-cut Carmen Marc Valvo gown, sleeveless, backless, and strapless, who discovers despite wearing almost nothing, she is shedding sweat like an entire NFL training camp, may equip the gown with small, discreet, jeweled clip-on fans and brooches up around the face (a new joint venture of Van Cleef and Arpels/General Electric). Done in emerald and diamonds, often looking like an amusing rooster whose tail is turning (and cooling!) madly, or a lizard whose head is constantly shed for a new one (makes a breeze), or like darling little jeweled vintage fans, these new pins discreetly circulate huge amounts of air, for formal hot flashes (see Figure A). A pavé diamond personal cooler "cuff necklace" (rumored to be by

Paloma Picasso/The Sharper Image) with matching pavé "drop-down fan" ear clips (Figure B) appeared in a Christie's auction catalogue, as well as a trend-setting casual diamond and ice cube neckpiece (Figure C)* and a rare, original Schlumberger-style "airflow pearl collar" with fabulous 11-carat cabochon emerald compressor (a perfect gem-quality air conditioner) (Figure D) and Audrey Hepburn's "faux couture" ear fans (Figure E). These comprise a new, exciting, investment-quality auction category (a category for which we show proposed auction catalogue pages): "Important Jewelry: Coolants."

Just-Discovered Facts!

The astute, soon-to-be-delighted Babe will be intrigued to learn that hot flashes don't just implode *within* her, lolling about, mindlessly wafting heat at her own organs, like drunk, passed-out blow-dryers. No, hot flashes scintillate *out* of her like some sonic musk, *drawing men* and *high-paying jobs, also reducing her energy bills!* Studies show some Babes experience a hot flash as a "high," a rush (just an intensely "barbecued" rush). There may even be street value to a hot flash, once Dealers price them out.

Studies show that today's Middle-Aged Babe does NOT think of a hot flash as the once coyly named "private summer," but rather as a sudden, free trip to the Bahamas, only without the hotel, the meals, the guy, the luggage, and requiring an SPF of zero! The New Babe *welcomes* hot flashes—having one, she'll generously hug a homeless child on a chill sidewalk, or turn them into a fabulous facial sauna, lowering her face into a Melitta coffee filter, running cold sink water below it, creating pore-opening steam. Enjoying Hormone Replacement Therapy (or newer Hormone Impeachment Therapy, where lost hormones like estrogen, instead of being replaced, are retroactively *impeached,* forbidden by law to rule the body again).

The Babe uses soy, Raloxifene, or new, greater products (introduced here first!) like Raloxifene mixed with Botox, or Raloxitox. This technology will ultimately bring new, cooling "menopausal face powders" to market. They'll warm and even skin tone *while* freezing the face and neck! No, the Middle-Aged Babe will *not* be the crash test dummy of her own hormones. She mentally *leaps over* menopause, not allowing it to interfere with anything, including having children.**

The New Middle-Aged Babe's Proud Menopausal Heritage and Fabulous Menopausal Frontiers

The New Middle-Aged Babe has come in on menopause at the right time: when it's hip. In ensuing chapters, we will reveal fabulous new menopause "symptom opportunities," such as: "Bone Loss Meds Causing Decreased Risk of Cancer and Heart Disease," "Menopause-Induced Elevated Sex Drive," "Ballet Dance on Point via Osteoporosis," "Menopause-Generated Replacements for Fossil Fuels," and (anecdotal) "Seemingly Menopause-Related Spontaneous 'Permanent Mascara' " (and brow waxes). Fabulous!!

---

* Already copied in CZ and ice cubes in department stores!
** See "What Is Late Life Birthing?"; "What Is Clomid (or In Vitro) Madness?"; "What Is 'Adoption'?"; "What Does a Perginol Overdose Feel Like?"; and "What Is Begging the Question?"

Following:

NEVER BEFORE SEEN PRECIOUS "MENOPAUSAL ADORNMENTS,"

available soon to hot-flash-engulfed Middle-Aged Babes—retail, online, and (date to be determined by Christie's) at auction.

Here, a prominent auction house catalog ad, responding to the Baby Boom's repeat pattern of growing older, shows some superb Van Cleef/GE-inspired pieces from their upcoming sale, "Important Jewelry: Coolants."

Figure A

Figure B

This lot (#258) inspired by the Sharper Image "Personal Cooler" in a rose gold choker (the "Change" necklace) with matching "drop-down" ear clips, charger included, would make a luscious "Coolant Jewelry" find!

Figure C

259

259
AN ICE CUBE AND DIAMOND NECKLACE

Composed of a series of ice cubes, with circular cut diamond rondelle spacers, pavé clasp, the necklace measures 19" frozen: 2" melted.
Signed: (sometimes) Paolo Frigito

Estimate: $4,000–$0,000 (if melted)

260
A PINK SAPPHIRE AND BLUE SAPPHIRE NECKLACE

Separated by diamond pavé rondelles, with an 18K gold bead clasp, the articulated cluster of stones is 17 3/4 inches, marked VAV.

Estimate: $20,000–$35,000

261
AN AVENTURINE CARVED BROOCH, WITH A RUBY-EYED, ENAMEL FROG, MOTHER OF PEARL SURROUND

This green free-form aventurine brooch, with an 18K pin and 18K frog with ruby eyes (approx. 5 points each), has a mother of pearl surround, suggesting a lily pad on a pond.

Estimate: $5,000–$7,000

262
A TORTOISE SHELL, LAPIS, SEED PEARL AND LABRADORITE BRACELET

With links alternating tortoise shell and 18K gold, this bracelet features lapis and labradorite stations, in natural form; stones highly polished, with seed pearl accents.

Estimate: $3,500–$5,500

263
A ROCK CRYSTAL AND ONYX CUFF

The onyx cuff, with rounded edge and an open back, is studded in front with a large polished rock crystal, in an 18K bezel.

Estimate: $2,500–$4,500

264
A PAIR OF DIAMOND, TURQUOISE AND 18K CHANDELIER EAR CLIPS

Intertwined circles escalate in size, each 18K: suspended within the four circles, alternately, are single old-European mine-cut diamonds, and cabochon turquoise carved beads. Approx. 3 3/7 inches.

Estimate: $20,000–$25,000

99

PROPERTY FROM ANNIE WYNETTE PINCUS NIARCHOS

 99

A CABOCHON EMERALD, CULTURED PEARL, AND DIAMOND CHOKER

Centering upon a cabochon emerald within a channel and pavé-set diamond and gold flower, powered by a no-drip compressor, flanked by pearl and pavé-set diamond bow-shaped 18K spacers, on a five-row cultured pearl and gold bead wide spring band, with an 18K yellow gold clasp.

Estimate: $15,000–$20,000

100

A PAIR OF TANZANITE AND DIAMOND EAR CLIPS

Clusters of marquise-cut diamonds and marquise-cut tanzanites, in a descending swirl, set in platinum. 1/4 inch wide, each.

Estimate: $20,000–$25,000

101

A TAHITIAN PEARL AND RUBY STICKPIN

Designed as a walking stick, this charming stickpin has a "handle" of a Tahitian pearl (12 mm), set in 18K, with a cabochon ruby gypsy-set base.

Estimate: $4,000–$5,000

Annie Wynette Pincus Niarchos, the menopausal socialite, rumored to be a muse of designer Schlumberger, is shown here in lot 99, an early "personal coolant collar" with emerald cabochon air conditioning compressor, prototype for (forerunner to?) the later, well-known "The Change" necklace. Before her numerous divorces, Pincus Niarchos worked tirelessly for AIDS and homebound-elderly causes, also hustled like crazy and God knows what all else, emerging tirelessly from beneath desks all over Wall Street.

Figure E

In an inconceivable mix-up, an aging, overheated Audrey Hepburn broke with her usual chic, to wear small fans on her ears, designed by Hubert de Giventilate (whose name she mistook for her beloved Hubert de Givenchy); she haplessly wore the fans in public everywhere, thinking them "de rigueur Givenchy," for some time.

Contraception

Which mode of contraception is best?

Younger Middle-Aged Babes and Babes who are relentless conceivors wrestle with this. Of course, the best means of contraception, the Uterine Frequent User ID and Password, old as monogamy itself, is infinitely reliable; we recommend it.

Happily, modernism has sped up the highway of vaginal intervention, providing new modes of birth control, though older modes are preferred by many. The savvy Babe must choose judiciously between them. Let's start by looking at one of the oldest, most reliable methods, which the Middle-Aged Babe may be glad to be reminded of:

The Diaphragm and Instructions for Use

Invented long ago by a man, the diaphragm is a good, if completely ridiculous, method of birth control, whose safety is without peer, but whose hilarious method of operation seems like something made up by the Playtex Rubber Gloves company in cahoots with Martin Short. Still, it is entirely reliable. The vigilant Babe, not wishing to surprise or ruffle the feelings of her uterus in any way, will be studious in her use of the diaphragm, as its accurate function is key to her pelvic happiness. Also, as is often the case with things involving the vagina, proper insertion is crucial.

Many Babes think they have this down, but the subtleties are dicey. Every woman can recall her first, meticulously followed, lengthy diaphragm insertion instructions.

But all women will have lost those instructions years ago. Or not looked at them for years. Others may never have read them at all, relying instead on friends on the other side of the bathroom door to shout things at them, without being too icky (i.e., specific). This is very bad: the diaphragm, inserted wrong, is worthless.

The instructions, though still lengthy, we have updated, shortened, and revised. We include here, then, a mistake-defeating copy!

These are for the Younger Middle-Aged Babe or the Still Able to Conceive Babe. (Other Babes may want to read them to reminisce—remembering the good old days when she needed a diaphragm, tried to insert one while reading yards of loud, crinkling paper, with her naked lover anxiously watching Johnny Carson on TV, inches from the bathroom, pretending not to listen.) Relive the verve and nuance of the splendid prose style of the manufacturer, especially given the circumstance (above). Like a treasured, oft-read book, the grace and diction of those diaphragm insertion instructions may have slipped your mind, written, as they were, with compassion and insight. We suggest that you recapture those moments alone in the bathroom, even if "post-diaphragm," and read along. (*Note:* Thankfully, our revised instructions maintain much of the prose flavor of the old ones.) Take a walk down memory lane! Here, our new, revised instructions for the perimenopausal Babe on how to insert a diaphragm.

AFTER YOUR DOCTOR OR HEALTH CARE PROVIDER PRESCRIBES YOUR OVO GROW-NO® DIAPHRAGM

Introduction

This booklet is to familiarize you with the OVO GROW-NO® Diaphragm and its proper use. Your doctor or health care provider will prescribe the appropriate size, which he/she has determined through the fitting process. This nonembarrassing process takes place in his/her examining room with the door closed.

LOCATION, LOCATION, LOCATION

Contraception with a diaphragm is most reliant on proper placement (location) and use of the OVO GROW-NO® Diaphragm with an appropriate spermicide, for prevention of pregnancy.

The OVO GROW-NO® Diaphragm is a shallow, dry natural rubber cup with a "flexible" metal rim. When it is properly fitted and inserted, it "boings" into place, like a sound effect in a cartoon, after which cartoon character Gerald McBoing Boing was named. Later models may go "Bing Bong" on proper insertion; still newer ones may say "Hello, you've got mail." Whatever model you choose, the sound will indicate the diaphragm properly covers the cervix and is being held securely in place behind the pubic bone and the rear wall of your vagina.

As a "barrier contraceptive," the diaphragm is designed to serve two purposes: to stop sperm from entering your cervical canal and to hold a jelly (or cream), which kills sperm that may manage to swim around the rim of the diaphragm. It may also deploy enemy ships filled with armaments to strafe, or even just sedate, sperm, depending on the strength of your prescription. Even stunned, sedated sperm are poor at fertilization and will float, dejected and despondent, around the birth canal, pointing fingers at the fallopian tubes and possibly laughing. Such sperm should be ignored (as they obviously don't like THEMSELVES).

The diaphragm should always be used in combination with a spermicidal jelly (or cream) (e.g., OVO GROW-NO® "No, Get Out of Here Now" Original Formula Spermicidal Gel, or OVO GROW-NO® "Look, Stay Out of Here, No Kidding" Crème Gelée," or OVO GROW-NO® "Anti-Sperm, Anti-Fungal Jelly Gelée Parfait Mousse, Grandee or Poquito," equally effective).

There are two types of OVO GROW-NO® Diaphragm: (1) The All-Flex® Arching Spring Diaphragm, and (2) The OVO GROW-NO® Coiling, Leaping® Diaphragm.

The All-Flex® Arching Spring Diaphragm is a molded, buff-colored, dry natural rubber vaginal diaphragm containing a distortion-free, dual spring-within-a-spring that provides unique arching action—no matter where the rim is compressed, it should just "go in."

The OVO GROW-NO® Coiling, Leaping® Diaphragm is a molded, dry natural rubber vaginal nightmare. The rim encases a tension-adjusted coil spring that provides for compressibility in one plane only, and that is the reality plane, the earthly plane we all occupy. However, when pressed, it will either slide easily into place or, more likely, spring out of your hand and fly around the bathroom like a creature from *Ghostbusters,* ricocheting off the walls, onto the floor, or into the toilet. Troubling, however, it is the better-priced of the two OVO GROW-NO® diaphragm products.

Your doctor or health care provider has chosen the one that best fits you and will be easiest to chase around the room or find, reaching into a toilet.

When to Insert the Diaphragm and Spermicide Jelly (or Cream)

The diaphragm can be put in anytime before intercourse. However, it must stay in place for at least six to eight hours after intercourse (depending upon which brand of spermicide you use and whether it deploys enemy ships), but the diaphragm should not be worn for more than 24 continuous hours. This creates an "insertion time conflict risk/result dilemma," as follows: if the diaphragm is inserted too early, a constant "boinging effect" may occur, as the rim presses against the inner self, loudly "boinging" during drinks, dinner, audible even to a waiter or passersby. As well—in putting in your OVO GROW-NO® Diaphragm early, a woman may feel she is presuming too much about the sexual outcome of the evening with a man she may have just begun dating. Or that such a man will, on discovering the OVO GROW-NO® Diaphragm already in position, think she is a slut. In fretting about this, a woman with an OVO GROW-NO® Diaphragm (the All-Flex® or Coiling, Leaping® type) may even worry this man can sense the diaphragm from across the table, or intuit its presence in her attitude, or that she is sitting funny, or that it is constantly "boinging" and being heard all over the restaurant. Nothing could be further from the truth. It cannot be overstated how much the man you are with can't see or hear the diaphragm. There is skin over it, fat, many, many organs, and usually a dress, pantsuit, or other "nice" outfit. And does the OVO GROW-NO® All-Flex® or Coiling, Leaping® type Diaphragm inserted before drinks with a partner one hardly knows convey sluttiness on the wearer? No, because the OVO GROW-NO® All-Flex® or Coiling, Leaping® type Diaphragm itself *knows no moods and strikes no attitudes,* nor (generally) does the penis. In this, they are well matched. And while no partner can "sense" the OVO GROW-NO® All-Flex® or Coiling, Leaping® Diaphragm across a room, certain men complain that during intercourse they can "feel" it. This, while uncomfortable, is mostly showing off.

The anatomy of the vagina changes during sexual excitement; the vagina expands and the cervix is pulled back and up. If you insert the diaphragm at this stage, the vaginal "landmarks" may feel a little different than usual, and, in addition to the changed "landmarks," there may be tolls required to be paid at this special time even if you have EZ Pass. Just be sure the diaphragm is positioned over the cervix. And where is the cervix? Many women are unclear on their internal anatomy, so we at OVO GROW-NO® are happy to explain them to themselves. Honored. As manufacturers of OVO GROW-NO® tampons and other tamponlike products, we have discovered the female anatomy is simpler, and way more convenient, than many women imagine, especially non–tampon wearers. Look.

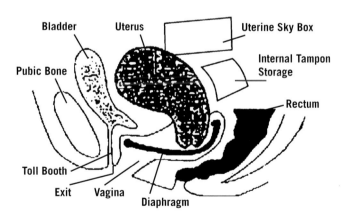

Bladder Uterus Uterine Sky Box
Pubic Bone Internal Tampon Storage
Rectum
Toll Booth
Exit Vagina
Diaphragm

Preparing for Insertion

Insertion of the diaphragm is simple, just in a complicated way. Cleanse the diaphragm before initial use by washing it with mild, nonperfumed soap and warm water, rinsing, drying, and ironing it carefully.

Empty your bladder (urinate) and wash your hands thoroughly before insertion.

Examine the diaphragm before use by holding it in front of a light to make sure it has no cracks or tiny holes. Do not stretch or puncture the diaphragm with sharp fingernails. Do not use if you observe visible cracks or holes. TO ENSURE LACK OF PUNCTURES: fill the OVO GROW-NO® Diaphragm with water or Hawaiian Punch, fold it in half, smack it hard between your palms while aiming it at a mirror. If water/Hawaiian Punch shoots out at your face all over the mirror and/or the diaphragm explodes, it will have to be replaced.

The diaphragm should always be inserted before intercourse, as inserting it at any other time will be a laughable exercise in futility. To prepare your diaphragm for insertion, you should put the spermicide into the cup of the diaphragm, spread some of it around the rim, which will be in contact with the cervix (entrance to the womb).

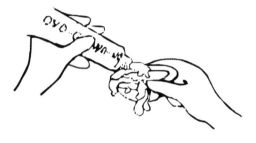

Be really, really generous. Once you have put enough on to be effective, put the same amount on over again, just for safety. While the product may "drip" or "ooze," making the diaphragm difficult to control during insertion, you will achieve a better spermicidal "sealant" film, such as the sealant film used in that Krazy Glue commercial by the man in the hardhat who glues himself by his helmet to a steel beam and then hangs by his head.

You can insert the diaphragm in the traditional ways (shown), while standing, with one leg up, squatting, or lying down. The position of the cervix and walls of the vagina will be different depending on your position.

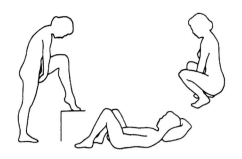

There are, however, more limber, aerobically trained women who may wish to try other, just as effective positions (see below).

INSERTING THE DIAPHRAGM

Hold the diaphragm with the dome down (spermicide up) and press the opposite sides of the rim together between your thumb and third finger. The diaphragm can be held from above or below. Separate the lips of your vagina with your free hand. Holding the compressed diaphragm with the dome down (spermicide cream or jelly up), push it gently in, along the rear wall of the vaginal canal, directing it backward as far as it will go *and try not to laugh.* Your index finger, kept on

ARCHING, SPRING DIAPHRAGM

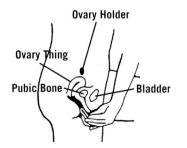

Ovary Holder

Ovary Thing

Pubic Bone — Bladder

COILING, LEAPING DIAPHRAGM

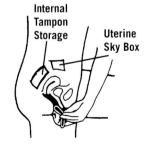

Internal Tampon Storage

Uterine Sky Box

the outer rim of the diaphragm, helps to guide the diaphragm into place and should keep you from laughing by poking you hard with its fingernail during insertion. DO NOT LAUGH, especially if the diaphragm leaps from your hand, careening around the bathroom, and ricocheting off the mirror. (Don't blame yourself. This behavior is the diaphragm's problem.)

Always insert the diaphragm as far back as it will go behind the mouth of the cervix. Then push the front rim of the diaphragm until it is locked in place behind the pubic bone. To test, press as you would a doorbell. If in proper place, as with a doorbell, you will hear a "bing bong" sound.

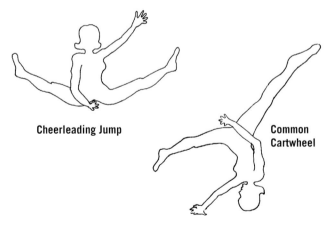

BING!
BONG!
BING!
BONG!

Probably Bladder

Bodily movements or changes in position should not dislodge a correctly inserted diaphragm. A properly fitted diaphragm should stay in place during urination, bowel movement, or a cheerleading jump or cartwheel,

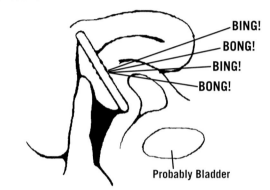

Cheerleading Jump

Common Cartwheel

which should be executed on a large football field before intercourse to check to make sure the diaphragm is in place. You may have to drive to the football field.

Preparation and Insertion of the Diaphragm Using an "Introducer"

Another way to insert the diaphragm is with an OVO GROW-NO® Universal Introducer. The OVO GROW-

154

NO® Universal Introducer is a more efficient, hygienic way to insert the diaphragm. It may only be used with the OVO GROW-NO® Coiling, Leaping® Diaphragm, in order to cramp its style. Although we are a company run by men, we are sensitive to the needs of women, so when confronted by them with the need for a method less complicated and difficult than manual insertion, for the Coiling, Leaping® Diaphragm, we respond. So here is what we thought of:

Preparing the Diaphragm When Using an Introducer

The introducer is a hygienic polymer "stick," designed to provide a stable "spinning surface" to aerate the spermicidal cream on the diaphragm, drying it, so that the introducer may insert the diaphragm easily, without slippage, and without the diaphragm flying (or Coiling, Leaping®) across the room. As well, the "introduced while spinning" diaphragm is more comfortably inserted and fitted properly into place. To assure that at least one (1) diaphragm goes in correctly, your doctor will suggest purchasing three (3) diaphragms and three (3) OVO GROW-NO® Introducers.

Preparing for Insertion

Insertion with an introducer is simple if you have ever done a vaudeville act requiring you to keep three or more plates spinning at once on the ends of thin wooden sticks. It should be emphasized: *inserting a diaphragm as a vaudeville plate-spinning trick is no more or less difficult (or humiliating) than inserting a diaphragm in any other way OVO GROW-NO® has ever thought of and is less embarrassing, although it will make you feel just as stupid.*

First, empty your bladder (urinate) and wash your hands thoroughly.

Then, place the hygienic polymer tip of three introducers in the center back of three diaphragms lying on a table.

Insert the amount of spermicidal jelly (or cream) recommended by the manufacturer of the spermicide you use into the folds formed on the top of the diaphragm (the cup side).

Now, lift the first introducer and begin "spinning" the first diaphragm, as you would a plate. While it is still spinning, raise the second introducer and begin spinning the second diaphragm. Now spin the third, *making sure, however, that the first two are still spinning.* This is challenging, but not as challenging as trying to insert the OVO GROW-NO® All-Flex® Arching, Spring Diaphragm or Coiling, Leaping® Diaphragm by hand, or trying to remember where, and what, your pubic bone is. If necessary, return to the first diaphragm, to ensure that it keeps spinning, then hurry to the second, then back to the third. You may have to run. When all three diaphragms are spinning simultaneously, choose the one where the spermicide seems most dry, but not cracked, rather, "spongy."

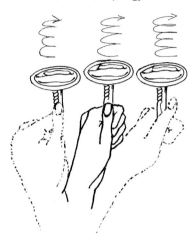

Inserting the Diaphragm When Using an Introducer

Being careful to keep the diaphragm constantly spinning, slowly introduce the introducer into the vagina. *It is critical that the diaphragm be kept spinning to fully aerate, and blow-dry, the spermicide.* Press gently inward along

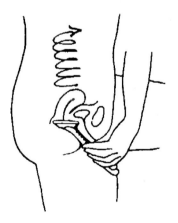

the rear wall of the vagina until the diaphragm has been inserted as far as possible, while still spinning. Don't laugh. Once the diaphragm is in place, you will feel the velocity subside. Withdraw the introducer and wait for the violent winds to stop. Using your index finger, check to ensure the rim of the diaphragm is locked in place, up behind the pubic bone. To test, push as you would a computer key. If in proper place, you will hear the vocal greeting: "Hello. You've Got Mail!"

To cleanse the introducer, wash with soap and warm water, rinse and dry by waving in the air like a conductor.

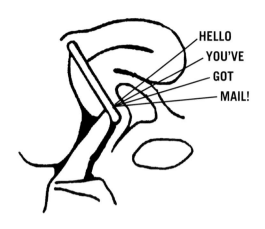

HELLO
YOU'VE
GOT
MAIL!

REMOVING THE DIAPHRAGM

Reluctant as you may be, you must remove the diaphragm six to eight hours after intercourse. Continuous wearing of a diaphragm for more than 24 hours is not recommended, especially as the "boinging" effect may begin again, becoming loud and public. Removal will also reduce the risk of a dangerous syndrome, "Toxic Shock," characterized by high fever, vomiting, and a rash, as well as another less dangerous syndrome, "Toxic Surprise," characterized by a big party and loud noisemakers, but only guests you hate.

To remove the diaphragm, put your index finger behind the front rim and pull it down and out. Avoid pushing it up, where it will jostle whatever tampons or valuables you may have placed in your Internal Tampon Storage Unit, and interfere with the view from your Uterine Sky Box, especially annoying if guests are present.

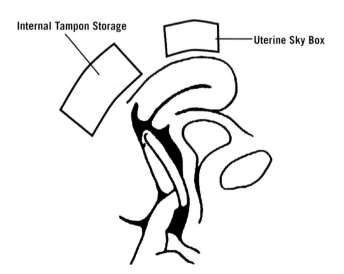

Internal Tampon Storage

Uterine Sky Box

To facilitate removal, straining down as with a bowel movement may help to push the rim down so that the index finger can reach the rim more easily. Groaning or grunting at this time is unnecessary, and juvenile. If suction is holding the diaphragm, this means the sex was really good and you may have a commitment. This suction may be broken by placing a finger between the vaginal wall and the rim, and "boinging" it against the vaginal wall a few times, just to give the diaphragm the idea that it's time to go. You may also simply puncture the diaphragm with your fingernail. Your doctor or health care provider will then direct you to purchase another All-Flex® Arching Spring Diaphragm or Coiling, Leaping® Diaphragm from OVO GROW-NO®, world leader in incredibly invasive, internal female products, and Inner Body Contraptions® no man would ever put up with.

CARE OF THE DIAPHRAGM

After removal, the diaphragm should be cleansed thoroughly with mild, nonperfumed soap and water, rinsed, dried, and ironed carefully. *Never boil the diaphragm or use antiseptic solutions in cleaning it.* You may, however, place it in the microwave for an hour on high, then serve it as a potato chip for a joke.

Where to Purchase OVO GROW-NO® Products

As you will surely want many, many more of them, we are happy to announce that OVO GROW-NO® products are available at all pharmacies, by prescription. The following OVO GROW-NO® contraceptive jelly brands for use with diaphragms are available without a prescription at most pharmacies and some grocery stores, but not Saks or Neiman Marcus or anywhere good:

OVO GROW-NO® Regular Strength "No!"® Cream, large tube, 3 ounces only
OVO GROW-NO® GROW-NO-NO® Extra Strength "No, No!"® cream, with applicator
OVO GROW-NO® GROW-NO-NO ® Prescription Strength "No, No, No, Go!"® cream, large tube, 6 ounces

If added vaginal lubrication is necessary, you may want to consider K-Y® BRAND Jelly Personal Lubricant or anything else you can think of.

APPLICATOR OFFER

For an applicator for use with OVO GROW-NO® GROW-NO-NO® products, send your name and address to: God, What Else Do I Need? PO Box 4498, Shopping

Center, New Jersey 10922-3346. Please print clearly. You will receive one applicator by mail; however, instructions for its use are available only by prepaying postage equivalent to the amount required to send a Yellow Pages–sized document around the world a hundred times. Offer good while supplies last.

Manufacturer

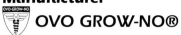 **OVO GROW-NO®**

OVUM-WORLD® MEDICAL INSERTERS
A division of GYNE-CONTRETEMPS PHARMACEUTICALS, INTL. Hubris, New Mexico 08774–099167428–2

14. From the Neck Up: The New Career Babe

The Babe Career concept, as close as can be reckoned, was a "now you see it, now you don't" idea dreamed up by the clearly hallucinating Women's Movement, having ingested a vat of LSD while watching a Katharine Hepburn film festival. Its central treatise? That "the Career Babe," employed by a company, would actually break "the glass ceiling" and go hang where the Men are, in the Money Wing of the Building. This, of course, proved to be a hilarious idea: that women, once Career Cloned, would simply "arrive" in auto-zip, male-sameness "equality suits," automatically receiving equal work, equal pay for equal work, equal job security, promotions, and pensions. Sixties women were off buying reflectors to use on the roof of the Money Wing of the Building before you could say "sexual harassment," believing all this! What a riot!

As we now know, no sooner did women leap out of their graduation gowns into their auto-zip, male equality suits and Ferragamo shoes than they learned: women in business were not to be men's equals. True, some rare few "House Babes," with a useful corporate genetic twitch, would be rewarded with Prominence in Her Field, others, with the fabulous "Keeping Her Family in Food," and many, many others blessed by "Just Getting to be Dressed up on a Daily Basis." Running shoes, handed out from a central dispensary (enriching Male-owned running shoe companies), *had to be worn:* walking to work, to not break female feet in heels so women could still type and crawl around on the carpet where their bosses "thought they dropped their pencil" and watched from behind, then home from work, so as not to break female feet, engendering undue absenteeism and unacceptably reduced carpet crawling. This, and the firm hand of then-all-male bosses (often placed on the firm hips, thighs, and buttocks of the new, uncertain Career Babe, wishing only to "please" and keep her "Career"), kept "Babes in Business" in their place, which was (at least while changing shoes) barefoot and pregnant (if firm boss hands had their way), a state not unlike that of the preceding Standard Female, "The Un-Career Babe."

Then What?

In such circumstances, many eager, talented, high-spirited Career Babes morphed into sad, disappointed ones, finding their "career" a thankless, life-sucking, ovary atrophying, godless imposition, stampeding chances at love/copulation/family (unless you met a guy on the bus *also* going home at 2 a.m.) with salary cutbacks, endless "early retirement" invites, and pensions lost somewhere in Management's desk. Amazingly, *even today,* "Women's Careers" are handed down like eensy, peensy heirlooms to teeny, tiny young Femme M.A.'s by Middle-Aged Babes "strongly encouraged" to quit (due to age, less cute, not spoken aloud, illegal), seniority (salary bumps, not spoken aloud, illegal), and most often "less pinchable behinds" (spoken aloud). These Babes are routinely shown out by male armed guards dressed as non-armed guards (often in aprons and nurse hats). This Babe can get a job again—but her seniority and benefits at McDonald's will be nothing like what they were at her previous employment.

Now What?

Many Babes "consult" (synonym for "don't work"). But most Babes prefer oxymoronic "Job Security" and actually "seek new employment." Amazing! Once "Fast Track," these "Cul-de-Sac Track" Babes might use severance pay to start a business! (Note: "Freelance," better—less time, adventure—but, example: one Babe became a "Freelance Anesthesiologist." She flies to various hospitals, filling in for anesthesiologists on vacation. So—Travel, New Men, what drawbacks could there be, she wondered. Well, here it is: she can't recognize her rental car *EVER. IMAGINE THOUSANDS AND THOUSANDS OF TIMES OF NOT RECOGNIZING YOUR* "Chevy Vixen" or "Ford Castrata" or "Dodge Impedia" or "Nissan Canasta" or "Toyota Quandary" or "Pontiac Pixel."

What to Do When You're Fired

Make a new résumé. Even if you just took a leave of absence to have kids, worked from home. Good resumes are brief, objective. Example: one accomplished Babe's first draft resume, composed by her, is shown.

Self-Employed Babes

Babes self-employed from the get-go are wisest. The Self-Employed generate multiple "Client Rolodexes," "networking" with "Business Cards" and "typing letters" in "Office Spaces." "Office Spaces" accrue to such Babes, as do secretaries, laptops, and faxes, the whole creating a sort of "Ambient Zen Boss," inducing an inner-body "Success Generator" (like the Dalkon Shield before they took it off the market) (this naturally occurring organ "kick starts" itself, when "good work vibes" surround it). "Need to Pay For Office Space Rent," "Need to Pay For Everything," doesn't upend such Babes, who come from a place of well-being that knows: at least *they won't fire themselves.*

FIRST DRAFT RÉSUMÉ

(Babe Name Here)

1996-1998: Chief Editorial Page Editor, *The Wall Street Journal*, 200 Liberty Street, New York, New York 10281

Duties and Responsibilities: To write, edit, and oversee the writing and editing of all editorial pieces run by *The Wall Street Journal*, representing the political views of *The Wall Street Journal*, discerned through frequent luncheons, breakfasts with luminaries in politics and public policy (which I hosted); also, to travel to hot spots, and cause others to travel, contributors to the Editorial Page of *The Wall Street Journal*, while overseeing the writing, editing, and all other cognitive processes of staff in the field (or office) yet appear always cutely dressed, creased, polished, not acknowledging the slime, muck smell of death in the air (in the office or the field). Also, to shut up, just shut up, when you return from risking your life and see that guy from "Weekend and Leisure" receiving "sample couches" from Donghia, goody bags from MOMA openings, flowers from "L'Olivier," as I quietly wash the blood from my person in the broom-closet sink, while attempting to rinse Passport.

1998-2000: leave of absence for pregnancy

2001-2006: extend leave of absence to "imprint self" on children

Suggested revision: this period, actually spent by the Babe driving in car pools, screaming at the kids to wear seat belts while "Elmo's World" blared from a CD over and over while the boys practiced puking, might, on her resume, be more attractively framed as follows:

2001-2006: *Wall Street Journal* **Transportation and Safety Facilitator, Domestic Division**
Duties: The safe transport of *Journal*-engendered future personnel/subscribers and critical support personnel and materials through difficult passages of upheaval, like when time virtually stood still as a Really Big Red Truck passed.

How to Start a Business Now

There are two types of severance-pay Babe Businesses: the "Bubble Wrap–Based Business" and the "Non-Bubble Wrap–Based Business." Except for the delightful "bubble wrap mindless popping for self-amusement perk," they can be equally enjoyable.

"Bubble Wrap–Based Businesses"

A popular new "Spare Room Career," these are businesses where the Babe sends Things wrapped in bubble wrap every day to purchasers. Example: "eBay," where "Special Things" are sold through hyper-theatrical "eBay auctions" (a clock ticks down and bidders wait until, say, 2:36 a.m. to score miraculous rarities, like a handkerchief from 1957 with a girl wearing a polka-dot dress on it). This highly regarded "girl handkerchief" must then be wrapped in protective bubble wrap, proof of its great value and fragility, then shipped. A windfall to Bubble-Wrap-Centric Babes who think Bakelite barrettes and fifties gold-flecked Lucite purses are intrinsically valuable "Things," though they often appear in other people's garbage—(where Babes may "score" them, sell on eBay in bubble wrap, ship at 100% profit!).

"Non-Bubble Wrap–Based Businesses"

"Fan out" (in your own body) to area Salvation Armys, Goodwills, Thrift Shops to "source" couture finds, resell at Consignment Shops to fools. See—all the good businesses have *not* already been thought of by Bill Gates and Sam Walton. Bat around other fine business ideas like "We-Make-Sheets-Into-Curtains" and (run ad in local classified) "I Find Lost Reading Glasses."

Other Second Careers for College-Educated Middle-Aged Babes

"To Begin"

Use the "Prostitution Business Model" but prostitute some less "God is just so buzzed" body part (the mind, the foot ["shoe model"], etc.). Well-educated Babes—with B.A.'s, M.A.'s, M.F.A.'s, or Ph.D.'s—and thus, few real world skills—rejected by IBM, Fidelity, Carvel, and Walgreens as overqualified, might consider: Exotic Dancing, Eyeglass Style Suggester, Freelance Closet Organizer, At Home Car-Detailing, Fashion Stylist to Bridal Parties, or whatever! *Note*: Work is on a "cash basis," flexible hours, minimal IRS intrusion—the rewards of prostitution without the wrath-of-God part *and* the prostitution part!

"Think-Forward Careers"

One must also "think forward," conceiving employment needs of the future. "Future-Oriented" Babe Careers to consider: Thinking up names of new medicines they will soon be advertising and singing about on TV. Random mixes of catchy "med-tech-y" syllables with zing, dreamed up by Babes, would constitute a "work sample." As there is no apparent relation between the product and its name, the Babe should be able to knock off a few hundred new TV medicine names while watching the Home Shopping Channel or reading *The Wall Street Journal*. Suggestions:

Asperteeni	**Alflexeral**	**Thigheviction**	**Rolontin**	**Centratabs**
Phlebacal	**Scowliminate**	**Nymphozing**	**Albutranex**	**Vagicontin**
Coppafil	**Lungbuff**	**Vivarivin**	**Dermaveg**	**Cepavil**

"Invent Fake Butters"

Done for years but never well, fill this need with a non-transfat, non-fat-fat, soft yellow glob, be showered with thanks, profits! To begin: go to Sweden, Norway, France, and other places real butter still is, taste, photograph, roll in fingers for correct color, consistency. Ten pounds later, return, invent!

"Buy Stuff Cheap on eBay, Rent Space, Hire Employees, and Sell It to People at a Profit, Taking into Account Your Overhead"

Once known as "Having a Store," this fulfilling all-new career *still involves bubble wrap!*

"Invent Hard Scientific Things"

Example: Develop new hair color, squirted out monthly, automatically, from within the head. Pursued by pharmaceutical researchers, chemists, this seems easy, if the Babe can just fit the medulla with a "spray mechanism," "hair color well," and "projectile drencher." Elusive, sought for years by the same crowd tracking "Big Foot," once found, it will shower the Babe Finder with wallet-cut-to-fit currency!

The Babe may have ideas herself, acting on them and failing time and again. Just remember: falling on hard times may soon become very chic. And the MAB is nothing if not a trendsetter!

How to Retire From Being Unemployed

Cut down, invest more! Club Hopping Kid Babes don't think of ordering in Bean Sprouts as "an investment" but it is. Experts see little performance from Bean Sprouts, see no future in them, don't expect them to "split" or provide dividends. Fired–Retired Babes must "spend-invest" to spread money and, even at this late unfortunate date, try to generate a "Retirement Cushion" (or Throw Pillow) (see "Finances"). How?

Retirement

A frisky post-war economy made life simple for the Middle-Aged Babe's Predecessor (and mother), the "Old-Aged Babe," who watches her investments fondly, like frolicking spaniels on a dividend-strewn lawn. Not so for Today's Babe. "Baby Boomers," of which the Middle-Aged Babe is one, are an entitlement-engorged group, who expected, like a trillion Gatsbys, to meander one day back to the Family Summer Palace (earned by them, themselves) and live out their days at at-home pool parties. Instead, Middle-Aged Babes recently speed-learned terms like "rollbacks," "bad divorce settlement," and other phrases meaning "You don't get the money." Social Security is even threatened. The Zealous Babe, however, has a plan to save Social Security, which she thought of just now, pulling in the driveway. Here's her idea:

The Entire Baby Boom Holds a Giant, Joint Garage Sale

We pick a weekend, have a federally managed, nationwide garage sale, run by *Antiques Roadshow* (online for questions from garages around the country on the value of certain Vinyl records, etc.) and the U.S. Department of Treasury (to collect, count the money, deposit it in Social Security's Checking Account). Everything will be bought for "Cheap Life Start-Up" by Generations X and Y and other lettered young people. They can buy our old sofas, toaster ovens, Bar Mitzvah suits, copies of "Steal This Book," Villager and Ladybug outfits. The hard part? *It will be hard to get everyone to agree on a weekend!* But we can—for as Babes know, *Woodstock was on a weekend*. Also hard: *Who letters the signs and who hangs them on a hundred million miles of telephone poles?* With Babes the biggest shoppers in history, inventory's high, and heady profits pooled will easily "boost the Social Security Lock Box." Help should come from "Ben and Jerry"—their socially concerned ice cream should be handoffs, like to marathon runners, for go-go shoppers.

Thus, even the sacked Babe can envision retirement.

Mike Todd (producer of *Around the World in Eighty Days*) once bragged he'd been broke, but never poor. What can this Generation of Babe brag? That they had co-ops, but never new underpants? Affording things, boosted by the sale (above), means phrases like "I'm completely broke" and "I'm really completely broke" won't be clever, ubiquitous new catch phrases like "I'm a wild 'n' crazy guy" and "Top Ten" lists.

Let's hope so.

15. Conclusions

"You only live once and usually not even then."
—MICHAEL O'DONOGHUE, 1940–1994

When astronauts first stepped on the moon, we civilians equally imagined them engulfed and incinerated by a virulent meteorite storm unleashed by the Moon King, or embraced and cosseted by a lush MGM-like orchestration of something like "We Welcome You to Munchkinland," sung by adorable, if crater-skinned, moon creatures, taking the astronauts' hands, frolicking and skipping with them toward a catered lunch, thoughtfully providing extra oxygen canisters and Earth-prefixed cell-like phones (should anyone wish to "phone home"). Yes, to us civilians (excepting scientists and boy scouts), each possibility seemed equally likely: this was, after all, the moon, boundless, limitless, in both size and intent, in its capacity to exhilarate or destroy, borderless, with no gravity (either a good or bad thing). In short, the moon was as unknown to us, in its delights and deathly rigors, as the Marx Brothers' "Freedonia." This, of course, was before we saw what really happened: the astronauts whirling into a Bob-Fosse–like pas de deux, somehow knowing every step with the locals, then going to see what witch they killed, and finally, checking in at the Lunar Marriott, where many of them (unimpeded by troublesome gravity) achieved triple-pike dives into the pool, often for the first time.

Like the moon, the uncertain surface of The New Middle Age cries out for Middle Age rovers to go there first, experimental monkeys to orbit The New Middle Age, followed by brave, former test pilots, trained in Middle-Age–like conditions at the Kennedy Space Center, to don protective suits, before us, and go check it out. Lacking this, we can only remember those great pictures of astronauts on the moon, ordering in room service, calling Sweden whenever they wanted, skiing in midair. Remember what a great time they had? We must do the same with this "bonus time." However long, enjoy it. However short, enjoy it.

I once went to Paris with my sister Judi Miller, she right out of law school, me a writer for *Saturday Night Live*. Ten years later, we found a picture, us, posed under some carefree red Parisian awning, full-length shot. I was delighted—Judi stared, then said sadly: "We thought we were so old and so fat, but we were so young and so thin." This, of course, was right, not just for this picture, but for all pictures forever. In this rich "Age of Oil of Olay," despite difficulties, uncertainties, Babes must (ever) enjoy their young, thin selves.

Grow old (or Middle) exuberantly. As my mother would say, "What else?"

—*Marilyn Suzanne Miller*

Acknowledgments

By now, I have as many live friends as dead ones. Each gets equal billing and endless thanks.

To my wonderful family for RELENTLESS, hands-on support, love, and superb legal services: my sister Judi The Lawyer, her husband Bill, my sister Joanne, her husband Steve, Tata Anna, Uncle Morley, Jacqueline Zagury, Michele Bass, Tom Bass, Shana, and Jonah.

To those extraordinary mentors who, with great kindness (and in the case of Jim Brooks, deep faith in the phone) first allowed my work to be seen and performed as written, I extend thanks forever. These people include: the great, beloved James L. Brooks, generous Garry Marshall, daring and kind Lorne Michaels, the splendid Joe Papp and Gail Merrifield Papp, and Joe Fox (the last two Joes, much missed).

To Paul Shaffer and his wonderful family, who kept me housed, fed, watered, welcomed, with a concierge, a private bath, and many fabulous emotional and physical comforts to cushion a rigorous period of YEARS, yes, YEARS, a million thanks. Love to them all. And for Paul's sensitivity (a friend and writing collaborator for thirty years), endless gratitude; also for his friendship and genius in guiding, encouraging, strategizing, empathizing, and being generous, protective, or hilarious, as the occasion, weather, or phone call demanded, thank you!!!

To superb writer/editor Dale Burg for hours of work, expert advice; to Gail Parent for encouragement; to Michael O'Donoghue for equal parts encouragement and discouragement; to Herb Sargent, who slipped my prose from NBC to The Publishing People in 1978; and to Gilda Radner, who taught me how many times to change gum in your mouth per minute, as well as unstoppable, superhuman courage, a thousand thanks. The same to James Gregorio, tireless lawyer and seeker of images and agreements; to my friend and writing collaborator of thirty years, classical pianist Cheryl Hardwick, who laughed in all the funny places; and to friend Fran Lebowitz, who, during that time, encouraged me, excoriated me to write, read my scripts on the phone to friends and strangers and set the curve for the Über Urban Female Humorist. More thanks to Veronica Geng, who encouraged my "voice," wore a perfect size six *and* was a *New Yorker* writer/editor for thirty years, and didn't brag about either. A zillion thanks to Bill Murray, a brilliant actor and a wildly (if secretly) generous, loving person, who has both saved my life and called me from foreign countries in interesting time zones at night, at least twice. To friend Judy Twersky, book saviour, also publicist non-pareil John Ekezian, great thanks. Also, to Susan Roston, Philip Bailey, their refrigerator, to the Chong family, Howard Mandelbaum, Peter Bochan, the Pook family, and Peter K. from Columbia, thanks. To Bob Pook and Karen Roston (dear, dear friend), both gifted artists and soul mates in overwork, endless thanks. And to Nancy Josephson the same—thanks.

Also, to Susan Moldow, who put out the funniest, most original book I had ever seen, the first *Saturday Night Live* book—a brilliant publisher, major thanks! And to Roz Lippel, who magically cracked the Scribner whip, rescuing and assembling this book with tireless devotion, many thanks! Also, to Kara Watson and Linda Dingler and the other Scribnerites I may have forgotten—thank you.

Love and thanks to Emily, Hannah, Drew, and Delilah.

And deepest gratitude to Dr. Richard Rabkin and Dr. Larry Norton, who even deserve more than that.

—*Marilyn "under a time crunch" Suzanne Miller*